This Isn't The Life I Ordered

Written and Compiled by Scott Francis

This Isn't The Life I Ordered
Written and Compiled by Scott Francis
Copyright © 2005 by Scott Francis, Integrity Publishing Company
All rights reserved,

No part of this book may be reproduced or transmitted in any form or by any means, electronic or mechanical including photocopying, recording, or by any information storage and retrieval system, without permission in writing from Integrity Publishing Company.

Published by Integrity Publishing Company
May 2005

ISBN: 1-59712-005-7

Photos by St. John Photography
Graphics on cover by Joseph J. Wadlinger
Illustrations by Kim Allman

Printed by Catawba Publishing Company
9510-103 University City Blvd..
Charlotte, NC 28213
(866) 549-0608 • (704) 717-8452
Fax (704) 717-8453
www.catawbapublishing.com

Printed in the USA by the Catawba Publishing Company

This Isn't The Life I Ordered

Acknowledgments

This book is dedicated to my Father. He was, hands down, the smartest single individual I have ever known. He once chewed out a guidance counselor who told me that I would never graduate from high school because of my dyslexia, "Don't ever tell any kid that again." Thank you Dad for believing in me.

To my Mother…one of the finest human beings on the face of the planet. She taught me how to treat everyone, no matter who they are, with respect and kindness. She also believed in me… Thank you so much, Mom.

To my Grandmother… who impressed upon me the importance of being a gentleman, encouraged me to be chivalrous, and inspired me to do my best.

To my Grandfather…who constantly reinforced the need for a higher education.

To my best friend, lover, and wife, Dede, who gave me unconditional love, typed, edited, and spelled seemingly endless words for me, and who had to hear about this book for over fourteen years. I could not have done this book without you. Thank you, thank you, thank you!

To my chief editor, Marge Preston, a woman who truly knows how to work under pressure. Thanks for fixing my "jabba."

And finally, to all the people who took part in editing, reading, critiquing, crucial legwork, and offering lots of encouragement… a special thanks: Wayne St. John, Joe Wadlinger and all my friends and family who supported me.

Preface

This "C" and "D" student, dyslexic, down to earth guy, had no plans to write a book. Even though I had become an entertainer, told stories from the stage, and had been approached hundreds of times a year by people asking, "You inspired me, do you have a book?" I still did not. After saying no and feeling inadequate that I didn't have something to send home with the audience, I finally got the message. If enough people are asking enough times, you should give the customer what they want. I had no idea that I, Scott Francis (the guy who spells dog, c-a-t), would have, even in my wildest dreams, been able to do that. I really think if I could do it, a "C" and "D" dyslexic student, than anybody with enough determination can do just about anything they set their mind to. Enjoy your journey.

I have studied success all my life. I don't claim to have all the answers. I have over 1800 motivational tapes, hundreds of books, and dozens of stories that I witnessed personally that inspired and educated me. The answers can be found.

This is one of the stories I personally witnessed. In Gatlinburg, Tennessee, some friends of ours were vacationing in the mountains with their twin boys. The boys, twelve years old, had the attention span of a gnat. They were panning for gold and gems. They took a quick look, found a couple of pretty rocks, and then went off to other adventures. Their mom, Tami, asked Dede if she wanted to do a little panning in the pile the boys left behind. My wife looked a little harder than the boys. She found two or three gems from the exact same bucket, big enough to have cut and made into a ring. The rocks containing the gems were not pretty and didn't have any special markings. She didn't really even know what she was looking for. In fact, the most valuable gems were hiding in the ugliest rocks. She had to dig deep to find the jewels.

This book is literally full of gems. The deeper you look, the more you will find. My hope is that you will find at least two or three gems that will enrich your life.

Foreword

About this book:

- People love stories
- People love to laugh
- People hate advice, but don't mind suggestions
- People like jokes
- People like to learn new things
- People enjoy inspirational quotes
- People like cartoons
- People want a fun and easy read

This is the book I wrote. Thank you for purchasing this book (tool) from me. It is both my hope and my goal to deliver many times over the investment on your part. Enjoy, and remember to read something each and every day to improve you life.

Multiple purchases of this book are available at a discount through our website:

www.MovingPeopleForward.com

The author of this book is available for speaking as well as entertaining (comedy-magic) engagements. For more information contact: (704) 535-0000

Table Of Contents

Acknowledgments i
Preface ii
Foreword iv
You've Got To Know What You Are! 1
Committed 100% 4
You Get What You Deserve 6
Humor With A Purpose 8
The Answer Was Clear! 11
It's Truly A Wonderful Life 15
Prepare For Opportunity(Will you be ready?) 19
Compromise For Your Health 22
Top Ten Ways To Reduce The #1 Health
Problem In The United States: Stress 25
How To Wake Up Feeling Great 27
Ideas To Start You Walking 28
Ten Tips To Help You Get A Good Night's Sleep ... 31
Follow The Leader(Great Leadership Skills) 35
More Great Quotes That Have Inspired Me 37
Simple Outline For Goal Setting 39
Example Goal Sheet for 2005 40
Staying Focused 43
The Way of the Eagle 46
God's Last Name 48
A New Year, A New Start, A Fresh Beginning 51
Where There Is A Will There Is A Way 56
Pistachio Overload 58
Let's Talk Integrity 60
Movies And Real Life 64

The Gift Of Forgiveness 66
Untapped Potential 70
Fair, Just, And True 71
Financial Success Is Everything! Or Is It? 74
A Little Story 76
Common Sense Isn't So Common 77
Reaching Out For Something Better 79
Real Magic 81
Full Bloom 83
Top 10 Suggested Books! 85
Teamwork In The Wild 88
Roadrage(Letting It Go!) 91
What's Best For Everyone Not Just You 93
Why Complicate The Simple? 96
Leadership Skills At It's Best 99
Seven Steps In Knocking Out Problems 103
Humor With A Purpose #2 104
Looking For Love In All The Right Expectations 106
An Almost Perfect Marriage 110
Feeling Good 112
Peace of Mind Is There For The Taking 114
Overcoming Some Of Life's Obstacles 120
True To Yourself 122
Looking Ahead 125
Good Communication A Must 128
Bound And Determined 131
Raising Standards 134
More On Expectations 136
Seven Major Don'ts At Work And At Home: 138
Stand Up For Something You Believe In 140
Attitude 144
Peer Pressure(Give Me a Break) 145

Low Self-Esteem 147
The Big Rescue 151
Seven Questions To Ask Yourself 155
Good Vibrations 156
The Magic Of Team Work 157
How To Get More Time For Yourself 159
Welcome To America 162
Customer Service? 165
Your Optimum Life 167
Sleep – How To Get It 170
Yadda, Yadda, Yadda 172
Caring Speaks Volumes 175
Reputation And Character 177
Get Rid Of Your Junk 179
The Power In Focusing Now! 181
Respect, How to Get It 185
The Blame Game 189
Oh Woe Is Thee 192
Getting One Over On You 194
The Scorpion 196
Life's Golden Rules 198
We All Have The Same Wind 199
Pre-Judging People 202
Turn Dreams Into Reality 204
True Friends 206
Misunderstandings 208
Why Me? 212
"Love It" Technique 214
What's Important to You? 215
Be Careful Where You Get Your Information 217
Clean Jokes You Can Tell 219
First Impressions 221

Unstoppable 223
Unstoppable Story # 2:
Dave From Savannah (The Power of Passion) 227
The Big Cover Up 230
Humor With A Purpose #3 235
Humor With A Purpose #4 237
Humor With A Purpose #5 239
Attitude Is Everything 240

You've Got To Know What You Are!

It was one brisk October night. In fact, it was Halloween night around 7:30 pm. It had been dark for a little over an hour. Trick-or-Treaters were coming to the door at a pretty steady pace. My wife and I, for the past seven years or so had been on the road doing presentations on Halloween night. So, this particular Halloween, we didn't know what to expect. A toaster came to the door, a scary-looking clown, a genie, a football player, and so on. I got a kick out of asking the kids what they were. Eventually, one of my neighbors and their two kids rang the doorbell. It was very apparent they were from another country and had never been Trick-or-Treating before. I said to the little girl about three years old, "What are you?" She replied with a giggle, "I'm a pumpkin," which was quite obvious. I turned to the seven or eight-year-old boy who was wearing a collage of mismatched items and asked, "What are you?" He shrugged his shoulders and said, "I DON'T KNOW!" His mom leaned over and said, "You've got to know what you are! Then in a louder voice as they walked off, "You've got to know what you are!!"

Her statement to her son was profound. I thought to

myself, "Wow! So many people have never discovered what or who they truly are. They wait far too long before they take the time to find out." Don't you find that the most successful people seem to know what and who they are? They have a specific passion, goal or purpose. Haven't you ever heard someone say, "I found myself?"

If you struggle to find your reason for being, I suggest that you take a day or two, get in a quiet place, and search your heart and mind to find your WHY, your PASSION, your GOAL... your place on this earth. It might be something simple like becoming a better father, husband or wife – It might be something far more complex and envolved, but knowing what it is will absolutely catapult you to a higher state of being. It will keep you focused on why you do the things you do and drive you forward. Once you find those answeres, you will be either working toward your PURPOSE or away from it. You will have a target—something to shoot for in this life. So aim high! You know the old saying: "Shoot for the moon. If you miss, you'll at least hit a star."

Magical Gem #1

Find your purpose now. Don't wait. Listen to your heart and GO FOR IT! You'll be glad you did.

*Listening
to your heart,
finding out who you are,
is not simple.
It takes time for
the chatter to quiet down.
In the silence of "not
doing" we begin to know
what we feel.
If we listen and hear
what is being offered,
then anything in life
can be our guide.
Listen.
-Anonymous*

Committed 100%

One hot day, several years ago, I was working as a comedian. I, along with two other comedians, was traveling across Florida from one gig (job) to another. We pulled over to fill-up with gas (for the car). One of the guys went to make a phone call, the other was pumping the gas, and I was just stretching my legs. Suddenly, a voice rang out from a little guy with a strong accent. "Would you like to try an orange?" I replied, "No thanks." I thought to myself that if I want to buy oranges, I would buy them in the grocery store. Besides that, at this point I have never in my entire life bought, nor had I planned to buy, oranges from a stand on the side of the road. The man persisted. He inquired with an orange in his hand and an outstretched arm, "Have you tried one of these oranges?" I had to say, "No, I haven't." He put the orange on the cutting block, cut it in half and in half again. He held a slice and said, "Are you sure?" I said, "I'm sure." As he took a bite, juice started running down his chin. I remember thinking, "Wow, now that's a juicy orange!" Undaunted, he picked up another slice and said "Are you absolutely, positively sure?" At this point, I didn't know. I said, "Okay, give me the orange." I took a bite and juice was now running down my chin. So, as I was loading the two bags of oranges into my trunk, he yelled out, "We've got grapefruit too." I said, "Get away from me!" That man was relentless! His commitment to sell oranges to me was stronger than my desire not to buy. Initially, his chance of selling me any oranges was zero, zip, zilch, and nada. I had no plans on buying oranges, not even with his strong commitment and belief in his product. I didn't stand a chance. He overcame all of his obstacles and brought me from a zero to one hundred percent sell in less than two minutes. Bravo! And thanks to this man for teaching me and others about strong, unparalleled commitment.

Magical Gem #2

It is said that man very rarely tries his very best. With 100% commitment toward a product, goal, or yourself, you will absolutely be unstoppable.

You Get What You Deserve

One spring morning as my wife, Dede and I woke up, she looked over at me and said, "Do you know what I want to do today?" I said, "No, what's that?" She said, "I want to plant some nice, juicy tomatoes so we can have some nice tomato sandwiches." You can tell she's from the North, cuz if she was from the South, it would have been, "niiiice, juicy, mayters." "You know the kind… they will be SO BIG, it will only take one slice to make a sandwich from one of those big ol' homegrown, juicy tomatoes." She licked her lips, "I can't wait!"

Once the big ol' juicy tomato seeds were planted we waited with anticipation for weeks for the seedlings to grow. After what felt like forever, a yellow bud appeared. A few weeks later… BAM! The first tomatoes! They were about the size of Tommy toes… you know, the little cherry tomatoes. We were thrilled! In the weeks that followed, the tomatoes would not grow any bigger than the cherry sized tomatoes. Finally, she said, "You know, Scott. I think I planted cherry tomatoes by mistake." I agreed. We never did get the one slice tomato sandwich we had dreamed about.

The next year pretty much repeated itself… well, at least as far as the tomatoes went. The same, exact thing happened. We had cherry sized tomatoes again. She went to the grocery store, read the package of seeds she had been buying, and sure enough, it read something like: Big Bertha tomatoes, firm, meaty, and delicious, unrivaled for their abundant growth and husky size. Apparently, the wrong seeds got into the wrong package. The cherry tomato seeds must have made their way into the Big Bertha package, which brings us to the point of the story: It doesn't matter what you think you're planting, it's going to produce exactly what you planted. Isn't that like us as human beings? We say we're going to do something and, in reality, do something else. "If you want things in your life to be different, you have to do things differently"

Magical Gem #3

You reap what you sow. For example, read this whole book, apply the principles, and benefit greatly. Try a little, get a little. Try good things, and get good results. Keep a close eye on what you actually plant.

Sometimes you've got to go out on a limb. Isn't that where the fruit is?

Humor With A Purpose

I attended a magic auction with three other magicians, of lesser talent than me, (I'm just kidding). One magician was a children's entertainer. One was a mind reader who performed primarily at private parties. The third one did family shows and close-up magic. I was the comic-magician. We were four very different types of entertainers.

It was just after the auction had ended and we were at the restaurant getting some grub. The children's entertainer, Mark, told us of a gig he had recently done, performing at the White House. Pretty cool, huh? That story led to another and another. But he was extra tired and really dragging. After a while we were all looking at him as if to ask, "Does this story have an end?" He was actually slurring his words as he was fading off to sleep.

The close-up card guy, Jeff, made his hand into the shape of an airplane and started making sounds as if the plane engine was sputtering. Eeeeh-eh-eh-eeeeeh-eh. I said, "Jeff, what on earth are you doing?" He addressed the person telling the story, as he said, "You need to land that plane, dude!" He was trying to tell him to end the story. We all laughed big time. It was hysterical.

The point of the story is that Jeff could have said, "Wrap it up." in any number of ways, but he didn't. He did it through humor. We all laughed and he got his point across. Plus, there was no malice, or bad intent behind his joke. I know him. He was just ending a semi-painful experience. For those of us involved, including the storyteller, Mark, we needed to be put out of our misery. That boy, Mark, just needed some shut-eye. Thanks, Jeff, for the laugh and the humorous lesson. This was just another example of someone using humor to alleviate an unpleasant situation.

Mark McCormick, who wrote <u>What They Didn't Teach You at Harvard Business School</u>, says…humor diffuses tension better than anything else. Using humor is a smart way to handle things that can be uncomfortable. As for Mark, the children's entertainer, he got some much needed sleep the following day and is reportedly back to normal speed.

Magical Gem #4

If there is a nice or humorous way to get your point across, use it. It is a better choice than the crabby, cynical, or hateful way. You will get better results and reactions from others as well.

A diplomat is a person who thinks twice before saying nothing.
-Unknown

The Answer Was Clear!

It was the end of a great summer. I had planned to go jet skiing with two of my five brothers. We were to meet at a lake in Winston Salem, North Carolina at a designated time. I picked up my watercraft at a different lake about an hour away from where we were supposed to meet, attached it to the hitch on my car and away I went. Well… not exactly! I had locked my keys in the car!

There I was, an hour away with no phone, no keys, and all alone. I said to myself, "I have three choices."

    A) I could walk two or three miles to the gas station, call a locksmith, wait two-and-a-half hours to get my door unlocked, not show up for my brothers, and call it a day.

    B) Kick out the little triangular window in the back of the car (how much could that cost, really?), meet my brothers, have fun, and worry about the window later.

    C) Cry like a little girl!

I chose B.

It was getting late and we were going to lose daylight in just a few hours. Besides, a broken window compared to a locksmith – it shouldn't be much more money or trouble? Right? I met my brothers and we had fun that day.

The very next day, I had a speaking presentation, so I temporarily taped up the window with a plastic bag and some duct tape. My temporary fix was not without problems. First of all, I had to listen to the rattling of plastic while going down the highway for several hours. Secondly, I was inconvenienced by having to vacuum all the broken glass out of the car, which seemingly took forever. You see, I didn't know that when you break that kind of glass, it explodes into about a thousand pieces.

When I called the car dealership about the window I was told their cost would be $238 – UNINSTALLED! Installation would bring it to a grand total of $328... if I decided to go this route. Calling the locksmith initially would have been a better choice at $45, had I known. At this point that wasn't an option. I felt really bad. I didn't want to admit to my wife or myself that I had made a really stupid mistake by kicking out the window and I decided I would save the $90 installation fee and replace the window myself.

Before I got a chance to replace the window, I got sick and tired of the plastic flapping. I went to Wal-Mart, bought a black plastic notebook, cut the cover into the shape of a triangle, and taped it up with good ol' duct tape. To tell you the truth, I didn't think it looked half bad! The problem with this is that it prolonged the window project. It became an extremely low priority on my list of things to do, because I could live with a pretty tape job. Yes, it did eventually get old, so I started to call junkyards to track down a used window. Finally, after about six or seven junkyards and negotiating a price, I found one for $30. I was pleased that I found the window, but not really happy, because $30 would have almost paid for the locksmith.

Now, I know what you're thinking… why not have a professional install the window? At this point it had become "The Principle." In my mind I thought, "The bigger the expense to fix the mistake, the bigger the mistake." Therefore, the less I had to pay, the less guilty I felt.

Finally, the day came when I had a few minutes to pop in the window, right? Not exactly. About two hours into the door panel, two bent pieces of molding later, and a cut on my hand, I figured out I didn't have the right tools to replace the stupid window! I called the Auto Glass place and they said it would cost $50 to install. Do the math with me: it was $50 for the labor, $30 for the window, the cost of the plastic notebook, razor blades, and duct tape, about five hours of my time, and $100,000 worth of aggravation. Fortunately, I did learn five basic lessons:

1) Find out which piece of glass in your car is the cheapest to replace (It's definitely not the triangle window).

2) Hindsight is twenty/twenty. If I knew then what I know now, I would have called the locksmith in the first place.

3) Know when to swallow your pride, admit you're wrong (you're not bulletproof) and let a professional do his or her job.

4) If duct tape is left on too long, it takes the paint off your car.

5) Patience is a wonderful gift. If I had had it at the time, I would have waited for a locksmith or my wife and none of this would have happened.

This problem that I created, because I was in a hurry, dragged on for two-and-a-half months. If I had been more patient, the problem would have inconvenienced me for two hours instead of two months!

Magical Gem #5

Consider all your options before making a decision. Impatience could cost you unwanted consequences. The right choice is sometimes not the quickest.

No problem can stand the assault of sustained thinking.
-Voltaire

It's Truly A Wonderful Life

Remember the movie "It's A Wonderful Life" with Jimmy Stewart? What a great movie! Oh sure, it's an oldie (black & white), but a goody. What a great message it sent. I'm sure you've seen it…the one where Jimmy Stewart played a banker named George.

Everything seemed to be going along fine for years, with the exception of a few minor bumps and bruises that life hands out. Then, in one twenty-four hour period his whole world came unglued. At this point, the character played by Stewart, George, got drunk and really desperate. He was about to kill himself, because in his mind there was no hope. He went to a bridge in the middle of winter, climbed onto the ledge, and was getting ready to jump into the cold, icy water. Suddenly, someone ELSE jumped into the water. Stewart jumped in to save the man. It turned out the man was an angel and jumped into the water to break Stewart's preoccupation with killing himself. Stewart finally confessed to the angel that he thought he would have been better off dead and said, "I wish I'd never been born!" The angel decided to show Stewart what life would have been like if he was never born. He saw for the first time all the good he had done by helping people. A lot of people's lives turned out badly without his help. The people not helped had a worse life, more bad breaks, and less opportunity. Jimmy Stewart's character saw, within just a few hours, the difference he made in the towns peoples lives. It impacted him so much that he decided he wanted to live again.

Most people don't realize the difference they make in other people's lives. For instance, if I said I'm going to take my clothes to a dry cleaner down the street instead of one in my own neighborhood, do you think it would affect that business? What if one hundred people each thought that they didn't make a difference? That particular dry cleaner would most likely go out of business. So, do you think, in a small way, you would make a difference to those cleaners? You bet your life! You DO make a difference, but a difference none-the-less, right? We make an impact on others lives every day. And yes, you do make a difference.

Just know this, you are making hundreds, even thousands of differences each and every year of your life. Don't ever feel you don't make a difference just because you cannot see the impact you are having on others. And yes, you could make bad differences. Be aware of what you do and who you are; someone is always watching. I believe it will come back to you ten fold. I promise. So, go out and try to touch just one person every day, in a special way with a smile, a hug, or a positive attitude. What an awesome feeling when the boomerang comes back to you! I encourage you to go out and make a difference! You'll be happy you did. You might even say one day, "It's a Wonderful Life."

More on Making a Difference

There's a man I know who volunteered at the men's homeless shelter every Thursday for three years to help out people in a worse situation. One time, this person went to a yard sale and got a big box of used socks… must have had forty or fifty pairs in the box. Did that guy make a difference? Maybe not to you, but to forty or fifty men with no socks, he did. This same man asks everyone he knows for old clothes they don't want. This way they, too, can make a difference to the men's shelter. This man says it gives him an "attitude of gratitude."

He says doing this service personally enriches him. Not only does it make a difference in the unfortunate lives of those living at the shelter, but a big difference in his very own life and attitude. If you don't think you make an impact, (positive or negative) you're sadly mistaken. There are dozens of things you do on a daily basis that make a difference that you'll never even know you did! If everyone followed this principle… it would be… A Wonderful Life!

Magical Gem #6

Contribute to your home, church, job, or community. It's like a boomerang; it will come back to you most of the time. Either way, everybody wins!

♦ This Isn't The Life I Ordered ♦

You better hurry I don't do this very often

Prepare For Opportunity

(Will you be ready?)

When I was 17 years old, I had an opportunity to go on a field trip with some high school friends. The destination was Sea World in Orlando, Florida. My older brother, Marc, was a camera buff, with all kinds of photographic equipment—zoom lenses, wide lenses; you get the picture (no pun intended). I thought to myself, "Hey, I wonder if my brother would consider letting me borrow his camera stuff on my 'Big' Adventure?" I couldn't believe my ears when he said "yes." I was so happy! Here was my chance to take some great shots of my trip and impress my friends with my newfound knowledge of cameras. I had never used a 35mm camera before, with fancy lenses to boot, so my brother showed me how to operate the camera equipment. But there was just one problem, the camera pieces were disassembled in the camera bag. The next day I left for the big trip.

We finally arrived, and boy was it cool! We saw dolphins jumping out of the water, an otter show, fed the seals, and on and on. We were having a really awesome time.

At lunchtime, we decided to find a shady tree and eat a sandwich. That's when "IT" happened. The park had really pretty peacocks that were just roaming around free. All of a sudden, out of nowhere, one of the peacocks flared his feathers. It was something I had only seen in a magazine or on TV, but never live and in person. It was even more rare than seeing a rainbow, or a politician telling the truth. You should have seen it! It was ten times better live. It was kind of like a post card of nature compared to the actual thing. We were awe struck. Quickly, I whipped out the camera bag, unzipped it, got out the camera, and one of the lenses, attached it to the camera, and started adjusting all the dials to get it right. While I'm doing all that, my friends were cheering me on saying, "Come on! Go faster! He's gonna go down; he's gonna go down!" Finally, sure enough, he dropped his feathers. What a bummer. We tried everything to get the fine-feathered friend to flare back up. We hissed at him, egged him on, everything we could think of, but it never happened again, at least not on that day.

More on Opportunity

One rainy day I was traveling through the beautiful mountains of Virginia. I stopped to buy some blank audiocassette tapes for my presentations. The rain stopped and the sun came out. As I was looking toward the department store, I saw a large group of people looking up at the sky. Some of them were pointing with their mouths open. I turned around and witnessed the most spectacular rainbow, bar none, that I have ever seen. In my lifetime I had probably seen over one hundred different rainbows, but this was the best one. I was really enjoying the rainbow and thought to myself, "I wish that I had a camera." I decided to buy one in the store. As I walked through the store to get the disposable camera, I kept stopping to tell people about the really cool rainbow that was just outside the door. I was excited. It could have taken me two minutes in all, but I wasted valuable time telling everyone about the wonder that was outside. This added two more minutes to the task of buying the camera. I finally got outside and the people, as well as the rainbow were gone. I was disappointed that I didn't get a picture. I didn't even get to just stop and enjoy the sight. I can only hope I see another rainbow of that magnitude in my lifetime. I should have just enjoyed the moment for the moment.

Magical Gem #7

Be prepared, so you can take advantage of opportunity, when it strikes, it's magical. On a side note, they sell throwaway cameras for people like me!

♦ This Isn't The Life I Ordered ♦

Compromise For Your Health

A few years ago, I went fishing with my Uncle Joe. "Scott, I think I found the best fishing hole ever!" He said, "I was fishing and I pulled in an eighty-three pound trout! It took me forty-five minutes to reel it in." That's when I interrupted and said "Uncle Joe, I don't think God makes an eighty-three pound trout." He exclaimed, "NO, I'm telling you, it was an eighty-three pound trout!!" So I followed with, "Last month, I was fishing at the Outer Banks on the North Carolina Coast and hooked something HUGE. It took over an hour for me to reel it in. It turned out that it wasn't even a fish. It was an old brass lantern from an old pirate ship. I got it onto the beach, brushed off the seaweed, and noticed that the candle was still lit, **THE CANDLE WAS *STILL* LIT.**" My Uncle Joe said, "Scott, I'll take eighty pounds off of my fish, but you have to blow that light out."

Of course, that is an old joke. However, what a point it makes. We have to make choices every day. For instance: WHAT will we eat today, not WILL we eat today. We live in a society that has two or three cars in every driveway, a mall seemingly every fifty feet. To be frank with you, a society that is spoiled. The truth is that we need to learn how to compromise. Not our values, but with each other as human beings. We would have fewer headaches, be less frustrated with people and situations. The bottom line is that we would be happier, healthier, and more well-rounded and balanced. That way, every one of us wins by compromising and getting along with each other peacefully at home and at work. Isn't that really what's important? What are you waiting for? Go out and compromise with someone today, and watch the smiles, and be astounded. I challenge you on this one. It works!

Magical Gem #8

Compromise with people, you don't have to win and come out on top every time. Allow others to win, too. You will be a happier human with healthier relationships.

When we bring out the best in ourselves we bring out the best in others.

♦ This Isn't The Life I Ordered ♦

Stress? What Stress?

Top Ten Ways To Reduce The #1 Health Problem In The United States:
Stress

#1 Exercise – Walk, walk, walk. Did I mention walk? Or at least commit yourself to some type of exercise that increases your heart rate for at least twenty to forty-five minutes, three or four times a week.

#2 Laugh – Laughter stimulates your cardio-vascular system, which releases endorphins and reduces tension, causing us to feel better.

#3 Let It Go – Don't let the little things get to you. Deal with it as it comes, but do not, I repeat, do not let things build up! Like air out of a balloon, let a little stress out at a time and you will never burst!

#4 Music – Listen to soothing music to help relax. Upbeat music can lighten your outlook and improve your attitude. Some suggestions that have worked: Yanni's "Reflections of Passion" or George Winston's "Winter" are really nice.

#5 Read – a good book will focus your attention on something other than your stress. Censor your negative intake; be selective in what you watch, read, or hear.

#6 Eat Smart – A good balanced meal, or at the very least a multi-vitamin, will increase your energy level to help you deal with stress.

#7 Sleep Soundly – At the end of the day, put aside all the day's problems. Promise yourself not to pick them up again until the morning. If you feel really stressed due to lack of sleep during the day, take a five to twenty minute "power nap" to refresh yourself if possible. Studies have shown that this amount of time is sufficient for your body to recharge itself for the next few hours.

#8 Hobbies – Enjoy an existing hobby or take up a new one. This clears your mind and gives you something positive to focus on.

#9 Complete a Task – Get an unfinished project done! This promotes a sense of accomplishment and will motivate you towards the next project.

#10 Take a Bath – Fellow employees will appreciate it! Just kidding! Start with warm water for about ten to fifteen minutes, and then gradually add cold. Warm water revs up circulation and relaxes tight muscles. Cold water stimulates nerves, refreshes, and clears your mind.

Stress Does Not Have to Control Us at Work or at Home

How To Wake Up Feeling Great

I discovered this by mistake. One night I set my alarm for six am. It was when I had a regular job (nowadays I am up at the crack of noon). I set the alarm to wake up to the radio instead of the buzzer by mistake. At six am the alarm went off and the radio started playing the Lionel Ritchie song, You Are. The song started playing softly from the beginning at exactly six. I was lying on my back with my eyes still closed "boom ta, boom ta, boom ta…Baby you'll find…boom ta…There's only one love… boom ta, boom ta …yours and mine…ta boom, ta boom." Before I knew it I was smiling while splashing water on my face. By the time I was brushing my teeth, I had started dancing around. I thought to myself, "Waking up feeling fantastic is possible." You know we don't have to wake up to, "BEEP, BEEP, BEEP" or "EEEEEEEEEE!" We have the technology and should enjoy waking up. Try it. Not only will you like it, but it will start your whole day off right!!

Ideas To Start You Walking

1. Start Small - You don't have to start off with a 45-minute walk on the first day. We all crawl before we walk. Walk one block. Walk two the next time, and so on until you reach your goal. On the days you truly don't have time for a full 45-minute walk, you can get by and still be effective with at least a twenty-minute walk. However forty-five is better.

2. Get Tough - One thing I do is put a Post-It note on my mirror that reads: "Walk. NOW." I also put my sneakers in front of the bedroom or front door. This reminds me of what I must do.

3. Stay On The Right Track - Make sure walking is on your priority list of "To Do's" each day. STAY FOCUSED in order to get it done and you won't "de-rail."

4. Don't Delay - If you put things off for too long, they don't get done. You will continue to find more and more excuses. Start today!

5. Combine Activities - Like instruments in an orchestra coming together to accomplish one goal; you don't have to just walk when you walk. Bring your tape player with headphones, sightsee, make your "to do" list for the next day, or pray or even meditate. Whatever works best for you.

6. You're Not Being Punished - Just focus on the benefits of walking. Sometimes you have to push yourself, but think how much better you will feel once you've done it. Think of it as something you have to do every day, like brushing your teeth, or using your seatbelt. It will make you less stressful, happier, and healthier. It even improves your posture.

7. Reward Yourself - Especially in the beginning. For example: If I walk this whole week, I will buy myself a new pair of shoes, or allow myself a piece of chocolate, or dessert, and not feel guilty. Remember, don't overdo the rewards, moderation is good.

8. Give it a Fair Shot - Don't just walk for two days and give up because you don't feel any better. Give it at least three weeks. Experts say it takes approximately twenty-one days to establish a habit.

9. Get a Walking Partner - Not only is this safer and more fun, but sometimes teammates can motivate each other to stick with the program. I love taking my wife with me; it is a great time to talk about those things you don't usually have time to discuss.

10. Just Do It - Why are you continuing to read this? With all these reasons, you should be out walking now. Walking works, please trust me!! Good things happen when we keep our commitments.

The choices you make today impact your tomorrow.
-Anonymous

♦ This Isn't The Life I Ordered ♦

Ten Tips To Help You Get A Good Night's Sleep

1. Choose to get a good night's sleep. You would be surprised what making this decision will do for you.
2. Food Intake – Watch what you eat. Specifically, stay away from caffeine, (your last sip should be eight hours before bedtime), sweets, or any food that is hard to digest – last bites at least ninety minutes or more before bedtime.
3. Music or Sound FX – Use music or a sound FX, such as a dream or sleep machine, to take your mind off of everything and help you relax. I use a programmable CD player that has a silent shut off. I do not recommend a cassette player that has a loud "CLICK" as you are about to doze off. The best sound FX machine I found was at Brookstone. Less expensive ones can be obtained at discount department stores.
4. Clean Area – A cluttered room is worrisome and reminds you of unfinished tasks. A clean room will give you a calm, relaxed feeling allowing you to drift off to sleep.
5. Read – Reading will help get your mind off the days problems, as long as your selection is not too exciting. Try not to read in the bedroom; you need to start thinking of it as a place to sleep.

6. Bedtime – Be consistent; try to use the same bedtime seven days a week.
7. Exercise – During the day, not right before bed, helps us to fall asleep better.
8. Temperature – Keep the bedroom cool. Most people sleep better in a cooler room.
9. <u>No TV</u> – Television stimulates the mind. You do not want this prior to sleep. Of course if you are the kind of person that falls asleep with a TV on, more power to you.
10. No Work – Do not, I repeat, do not bring work or problems to the bedroom. Take your mind off of them with music, sound, or thinking of something relaxing or peaceful.

If you are still having trouble, visit a sleeping disorder clinic.

Whenever you get the urge to exercise, lie down. If you're lucky, the urge will pass.
-Rodney Dangerfield

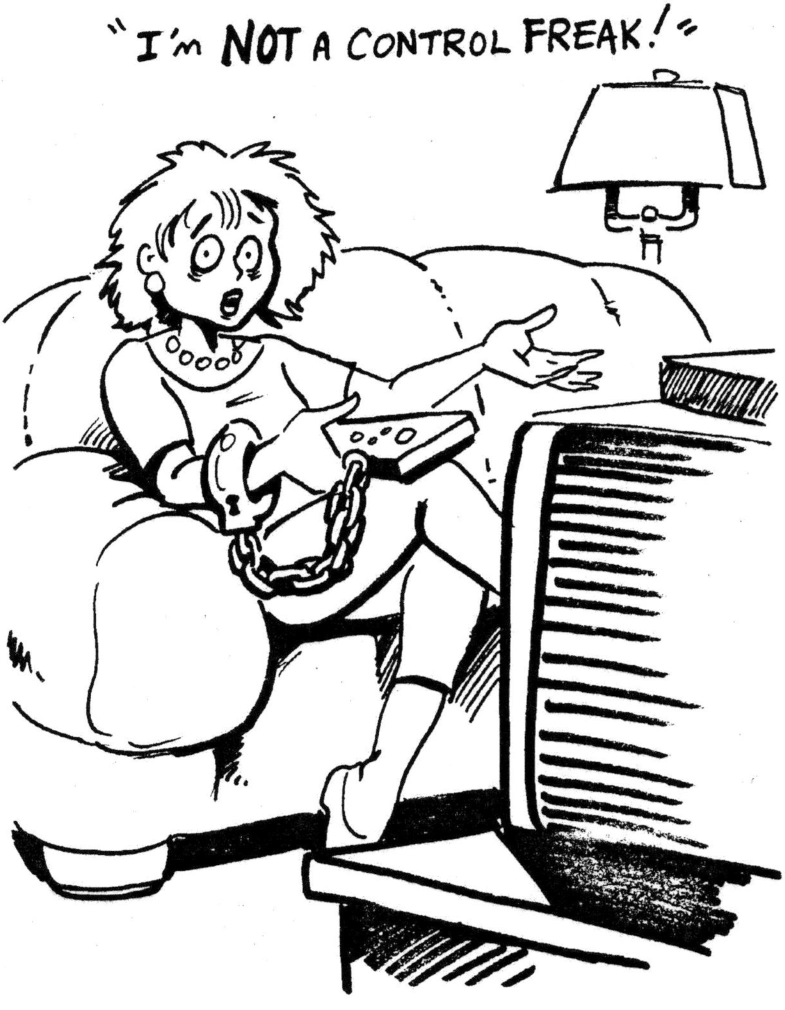
"I'm NOT A CONTROL FREAK!"

♦ This Isn't The Life I Ordered ♦

Who's in charge here anyway?

Follow The Leader
(Great Leadership Skills)

Don't ever confuse effort with results. Success does not come easy. Enhanced leadership skills – Are you willing to pay the P.R.I.C.E.?

Purpose
    Believe in what you are doing.
    Have a purpose – know your "why."
    Set out to make a difference – don't just collect a check.
    Keep things simple and direct.

Relating
    Stop, think, and then comment.
    Involve people – they are your biggest assets.
    Remember, anger manages everything poorly.
    Don't dwell on the past, the past is over.

Think like a winner, act like a winner, and look like a winner.
    People love to work with winners.

Integrity
    Honesty is the only policy.
    Be fair to all.
    Be an honorable person in your work ethics.
    Respect everyone – you heard me, everyone!

Compromise
    Compromise on critical or important issues, but be flexible

and strive for good rapport with associates.
Admit when you are wrong. We all have "feet of clay."
A diamond with a flaw is better than a stone that is perfect.

Enthusiasm
  Is the highest paid trait we have.
  Goal setting – paint the picture. Remember we think in pictures.
  Go for a record – it gives everyone something to shoot for. Remember to stay enthusiastic. Take care of your stress and get plenty of rest. Vince Lombardi once said, "Fatigue makes cowards of us all."

The people who get on in this world are the people who get up and look for the circumstances they want, and, if they can't find them, make them.
-George Bernard Shaw

More Great Quotes That Have Inspired Me

Great minds have purposes, others have wishes.
Washington Irving

One of the best ways to persuade others is with your ears – by listening to them.
Dean Rusk

I was successful because you believed in me.
Ulysses S. Grant to Abraham Lincoln

A man travels the world over in search of what he needs and returns home to find it.
George Moore

Most of the trouble in the world is caused by people wanting to be important.
T.S. Elliot

Truth is truth no matter where you find it.
Anonymous

Do you prefer that you be right or happy?
Anonymous

Patience is needed with everyone, but first with ourselves.
Saint Francis De Sales

We are confronted with insurmountable opportunities.
Pogo

Fall seven times, get up eight.
Japanese proverb

Simple Outline For Goal Setting

- Be absolutely clear in what you want. Be specific.
- Be realistic.
- Focus on your results, not your flaws.
- Set deadlines to make the goal more realistic.
- Plan how to reach your goals. You will be surprised at how much further you will go.
- Start small, and then build.
- Know your "why."
- Personalize your goal with details.
- Forget the past. What are you doing right now?
- Share your goal with others. Their involvement and update questions make you committed to follow through.
- Do something every single day to get you closer to your goal.
- Live your dreams, I do and you can too!!

"Obstacles are those frightful things you see when you take your eyes off your goals.
-Anonymous

Example Goal Sheet for 2005

This is just an example of a goal sheet. It is different for everyone. Write your goals down, and the steps you need to take to achieve them. Do something each and every day to move closer to your goals and watch what happens.

1. Genuinely Enhance Our Walk With God.
   - One hour a day in prayer or devotional
   - Pray when we wake – commit each day to God
   - Pray before we sleep – thank God for that day
   - Read one chapter of the Bible daily
   - Always thank God for the meals that have been provided

2. Enrich Our Marriage
   - Pray for each others needs
   - Attend at least one or two marriage seminars per year
   - Pray for inspiration
   - Attitude is everything
   - Treat each other like gold
   - Do one nice deed daily
   - Give at least one sincere compliment a day
   - Stare into each others eyes for one solid minute.

(You'd be surprised. Some days you feel as though you don't even have that minute.)

3. Increase Our Income to $xxxxxx a year
   - Be on time
   - Marketing Mondays six hours
   - Minimum of two hours every day on business calls
   - Read at least two hours a day on business topics
   - Listen to one tape a day – motivational or sales
   - FOLLOW-UP – stop throwing so much work away

4. Exercise
   - Walk at least every other day for a minimum of twenty to forty-five minutes
   - Play more outside sports together – tennis, roller-blading, etc.

5. Eat Properly
   - Take vitamins daily
   - Eat more balanced meals
   - Eat fruit or raw veggies as snacks

6. Get Enough Sleep
   - Bedtime at 11 pm
   - Lights out at 12 am
   - Up at 9 am every day

7. Have a Positive Attitude
   - Find something positive in everything
   - Say only good of others
   - If you don't have something nice to say, say nothing
   - Bite your tongue if it helps
   - Remember if you throw dirt at someone you lose ground

We always have time for the things we put first

Staying Focused

My wife, Dede, and I have been doing this daily checklist for years with great results. This particular list, on the following page, was designed with our specific needs, areas we should focus on daily for personal growth and to grow our business. Set up you own list for whatever works for you. Adapt what you want, and leave what you don't need, it's that simple.

I am so forgetful. All I know is that when I follow a daily chart I do better. I have a hard time remembering everything I need to do. Not just mundane tasks like taking a vitamin, or hanging the tub mat back up so it will dry, but also activities that will help me grow personally and professionally.

Dede, and I also have a little contest going with the daily to do checklist. The one with the most checks, stars, dots, stickers, or whatever you mark your chart with, at the end of the week (honesty is essential), is the winner and gets two things. #1 buy a prize like a CD or a new pair of jeans #2: you know that project that would take about an hour that you have been trying to get your spouse to do? If you win, they have to do it right away! This becomes a win–win situation. The real win is that you focused on the activities on the chart and got that much closer to achieving your goals. It's fun and it works!

♦ This Isn't The Life I Ordered ♦

Example Sheet – Daily Essential Checklist
Again, remember, it's different for everyone.

	Monday	Tuesday	Wednesday	Thursday	Friday	Saturday	Total
Pray – 15 min.							
Pray – 30 min.							
Short meeting							
Exercise/Walk 20 min.							
Fun/Exercise 45 min.							
Vitamin							
Read – 30 min.							
Read – 1 hour							
Business calls – 2 hours							
Cold calls – 1 hour							
Practice/business/pprwk							

Example

♦ 44 ♦

Example

Task														
Tape – one side														
Tape – one tape														
Organize – ½ hour														
Organize – 1 hour														
Fix-it/Run house – ½ hr														
Fix-it/Run house – 1 hr														
Pray/Devotional														
Floss														
Whitening/Sew – 1 hr														
Water – 40 ozs.														
In Bed – 11 pm														

You make your habits, then your habits make you!! Good things happen when we keep our commitments!!

The Way of the Eagle

Unrivaled Belief System

1. Have a definite vision, purpose, or goal. If you make everything important, then nothing is important.
2. Make good choices, develop great habits, and stay focused. Ask yourself, "Will it better serve my purpose?" If it doesn't, don't do it.
3. Help and encourage other people to become the very best they can be.
4. Hang around other eagles. You would be surprised at the results from this one step alone.
5. Always have something to look forward to it keeps life exciting.
6. Keep in constant touch with God, friends, and family and you will always have support from somewhere.
7. Be 100% committed to your cause. It will make a big difference!!

Do these 7 Steps and become Unstoppable! Success is different for everyone… What's success to you?

Magical Gem #9

Being an Eagle takes some effort on your part, but it will be well worth it! Become an Eagle. To be an Eagle you may not always be popular. Ask yourself, is the majority always right? You may be the only one that is right. Soar high, become an Eagle. You will be glad you did. I don't think I really have to say this, but this world of ours could use a few more Eagles. Don't you agree?

You can't control others, you can control your reaction to others.

God's Last Name

In the summer of 1983, I was twenty-three years old and in the remodeling business. I was young, anxious, and excited about buying my first brand-spanking new vehicle. Until this time, I always bought used cars and trucks. So, you can imagine my excitement about getting a new truck for my business that wouldn't break down all the time. I think I made my point. I WAS EXCITED!!

I looked at new trucks for weeks. Finally, I made a decision. I was at the dealership in the small negotiating cubicle (you know the one I mean). We had just agreed on price, model, and options. I had the pen in my hand and was, literally, seconds away from signing and making it a done deal. To my shock and amazement, the salesman selling me the truck started saying G_ _ D_ _ _ this and G_ _ D_ _ _ that. I glanced over at my girlfriend's father, who had accompanied me to help negotiate a better deal and not allow me to be taken. I said "I really don't want to buy a truck from a guy who talks like this and takes the Lord's name in vain." I stood up and said to the salesman, "thanks anyway" and left. I don't know if he ever made that mistake again. Let's hope not.

My only comfort would be that he told other salespeople this story; especially the ones that choose to talk like that in front of the customers. In my opinion, he blew it. He offended me, my girlfriend's father, and I think he would have offended anyone who believed in God. I am a very tolerant person and don't get offended easily. There are very few things that will offend me, but that is one of them. Since we are on this subject, let's just get it over with and step on a few toes. Not only is giving God a new last name offensive, but also so is profanity, dirty jokes, lying, and cheating. There is no room for this, especially in sales.

If you curse, you will always have to wonder if you may have lost a sale. If you lie and get caught, you look like a total jerk. What happens if you tell dirty jokes to the boys and only have one clean joke for your customers? Do you sweat bullets because you only have dirty ones to tell? You are probably in trouble. Make it a habit to tell clean jokes so that you never ever have to worry about offending a customer. This technique will most likely increase your sales. I know I probably stepped on some toes, and you probably think I am pointing at you. Trust me, I am not a "Pollyanna." However, look at it this way: while I am pointing at you, I have three fingers pointing back at me. I need to listen to this just as much, if not more, than you. I am sure that at one time in my life I lost a sale or two because of the way I talked and the jokes I told. I guess what I am saying is, it is just a learning process. Some of us wake up at twenty-five, some at forty or even fifty, and some never do.

Magical Gem #10

Make the decision to stop cursing and telling dirty jokes. It will absolutely raise the quality of your life. You never know, you might open more doors and make more opportunities, try it!

Many receive advice, only the wise profit from it.
-Syrus

A New Year, A New Start, A Fresh Beginning

Here it is 1:28 am New Year's Eve. Life is a funny and wonderful thing, chock-full of good times, bad times, and plenty of mistakes. The cool thing is, we can start over anytime we choose, no matter what the error. In the movie <u>Anne of Green Gables</u>, Anne says, "tomorrow is fresh with no mistakes in it." Do you know what a privilege it is to be able to do that? To start fresh at any moment we decide? In the most abundant country in the world, with that kind of mindset and that kind of attitude, we should try all kinds of adventures. Of course, in my opinion, it should be legal or at least okay with our maker. I don't know, I can't speak for you, but I have all kinds of inventions, places of travel, idea's, etc. that I would like to try, that make life fun and interesting.

When I see people that are bored with life it bothers me. If you have a boring marriage, do something about it. If you hate the financial situation you are in, again, do something about it. Don't expect others or any thing to dictate your life, your job…be the very best you can be. If you don't, you are only cheating yourself. And why on Earth would you want to cheat yourself?

Everybody gets down and gets the blues occasionally or even sometimes temporarily depressed. If this happens to you, take yourself out of the equation. Focus on helping others. Trust me, this really works. You will soon learn there is always somebody worse off than you. Always. It's called picking yourself up by the bootstraps, and snapping out of it. My good friend from Iran, whose name is Hamid, says a popular saying in his country goes something like this: "He is a person who can pull his own rug out of the river" (meaning they can hold their own). When they wash the Persian rugs at the river they get wet and extremely heavy. This person shows he can pull it out on his own without help indicating he is strong and able. That's not to say you can't ask for help. Did you ever hear the saying there are people who let it happen, people who watch it happen, and then there are those people who make it happen? I'm just trying to say, don't let things happen, make them happen! There is a huge difference. There are those people who take charge of their own life. There are those who do know where they are headed. They are usually happy people. Why? Because, again, they have a purpose, a goal, a target, something to look forward to…they become the Happy Human. So know this: whatever situation you find yourself in, know in your heart and mind, that tomorrow is a new day fresh with no mistakes. So…take the plunge and make a difference.

I believe the happiest people on Earth are not people without problems. They are people who know how to solve their problems.

Real Life Reoccurring Problems Solved

Example: 1

We had a scissors drawer located in the kitchen. My wife and I always, always, put the scissors back exactly where they belonged, NOT! Let me rephrase that, we sometimes, no, no… let's be real. We never put them back. For some reason or another the scissors were always lost. We both decared that we had returned them when last we had used them. One day I decided to solve this little problem. I went to Wal-Mart and bought seven pairs of scissors. You heard me, seven pairs of scissors, all with different colored handles and in different sizes. I had one in the office, one in my magic room to work on props, one in the kitchen, etc., etc. For thirty dollars the problem was solved.

Example: 2

When I first got married, I realized my wife's monthly friend visited and brought pain with her. My wife says when this so-called "friend" (wink, wink) comes to visit her she needs pain relievers in the form of ibuprofen. She was famous for misplacing the ibuprofen on a monthly basis, and the problem quickly got old. During that monthly time, she would look at me with bug eyes and say, "Where are those #@$%!!*&#@ pain killers?" I start acting out a scene straight from the Keystone Cops.

♦ This Isn't The Life I Ordered ♦

I would jump up in the air and run around like a chicken with my head cut off trying desperately to find her pain relievers. I decided to solve this particular problem by attaching an elastic string to the kitchen medicine cabinet and duct taping the ibuprofen to the string. It was kind of like the bank pen principle with a chain attached to keep it from walking away. Thus, she could never misplace those pills again. Now, it's possible that she could just rip the pill jar off of the string, but it's a constant reminder to her to not walk away with the pain relievers. That ensures they will definitely, and for sure, be there the next time she is in dire straits. This solution has worked for over ten years now. Problem solved. Next!!

Magical Gem #11

Sometimes we need to stop and think. We get wrapped up in the problem when we should be thinking about coming up with a solution.

Where There Is A Will There Is A Way
(Excuses, excuses? Get Real!)

About twenty years ago when I was still living at home with my mom, dad, and four brothers, we had a slight problem in the downstairs bathroom. The drainpipe, I think they call it the p trap (a "u" shaped pipe), was dripping about every three to four seconds. Once a week a bucket had to be emptied out. My mom asked my dad to look at it, and he could not stop the leak. Then she asked each one of the brothers, who were now old enough to fix it, to look at the problem. Each and every one of us said it needed a plumber; it couldn't be stopped. The drip could not be stopped…

My mom was somehow the person nominated to empty the bucket. Of course there was no motivation for us to fix the drip! We didn't empty the bucket. She said, "You mean to tell me out of the six of you, you can't stop that leak?" Our excuse, because that's all it was, was "we are not plumbers." Of course, this was still a cop-out. My mom said, "Then I will take a look at it." We all laughed and said, "Good luck." Then ten minutes later we peeked in to see what she was doing. She was starting to wrap the dripping drainpipe with black electrical tape. Round and round she wrapped. We laughed and laughed and said, "No way will that hold." Eight years later it finally had to be replaced. The story taught me two valuable lessons. #1 The majority is not always right. #2 Where there is a will, there is a way. Thanks Mom, you're my hero once again!

Magical Gem #12

If you want something bad enough, you will make it happen. She made it happen because she focused and never took her eyes off her goal.

Do not follow where the path may lead. Go instead where there is no path and leave a trail.
-Anonymous

Pistachio Overload

Too much of a good thing can be detrimental to your enjoyment. Allow me to explain. I love un-dyed pistachios second only to cashews. My wife and I will occasionally buy a four-pound bag at one of these warehouse type super stores. A four-pound bag will last about two months when shared with friends and family when they come to visit.

One day my wife, Dede, and I noticed a two-pound bag without the shells. You know, all the work of cracking and de-shelling the nuts had already been done for your eating enjoyment. We read that a two-pound bag unshelled was the equivalent to a four-pound bag with the shells. We knew that would be more convenient, and we wondered if it would be better. A couple of days later I did my own experiment to answer that question.

I took the shells off fifty or so pistachios without eating them (a very hard task to do) and set them aside. I then ate them all at once. It was a pistachio overload. What a revelation. My enjoyment level went from a 9 or a 10 (on a scale from 1-10 with 10 being the highest) based on the way I usually eat pistachios (shell on, one at a time) to about an enjoyment level of only a 1 or 2 based on shoving them in my mouth all at once.

I thought I might have enjoyed the convenient already shelled pistachios much more. The exact opposite occurred. I enjoyed them less. Actually, I was shocked to discover that. Maybe it's better to crack them open one at a time and eat them so you can enjoy the fruits of your labor, instead of being overloaded with a good thing.

Boy did I learn something: I will never ever, ever buy the two-pound bag already shelled. Trust me when I say, it was simply not as good. So, once again, I proved that too much of a good thing can make it not such a good thing anymore. I also proved that balance is important. That's something we all can benefit from.

Okay, okay, I went too far with the pistachios, which reminds me that I don't want to see pistachios for a while, at least a day or two.

Magical Gem #13

Always strive for balance in your life. Too much of a good thing can be bad. Its good to work for what you get, you appreciate it more.

Nothing in life is to be feared it is only to be understood.
-Marie Curie

Let's Talk Integrity

One person put it this way when speaking about integrity, "It's what you do when nobody is watching," doing the right, honest, and honorable thing.

One summer several years ago, I was working in San Francisco at a three day trade show when I witnessed something a little shocking and disturbing. I was appalled, to say the least. Now to some people this next item might not be shocking, might not even be a big deal. And if it doesn't shock you, maybe you ought to check "thine own" integrity.

This 70 million dollar company wanted leads (names and addresses of potential clients) at the trade show to increase sales. They were giving away some great prizes: computer software, an organizer, and a real nice jam box. They collected business cards and put them in a bowl. There must have been hundreds of leads in the form of business cards at the end of those three days.

One particular potential future client (trade show attendee) really liked one of the prizes. During the three days of the trade show, he would stop by periodically and ask when they were picking a winner. The person in charge of our booth would tell him they would do it in just a little while, never committing to a specific time. So when the man returned again, for the third or fourth time, asking when they were going to pick a winner, the boss at our booth said, "okay, at 4:30 pm. We will pick a winner out of the fish bowl at 4:30 pm" (an hour-and-a-half later). The guy said, "Great, I'll be back at 4:30 pm."

As soon as the guy got out of sight, the boss and assistant took the fish bowl to the back of the booth out of sight of the trade show attendees and dumped out the contents on a table. They started to go through the leads and said, "Let's see, who do we want to win? I think it should be someone that buys from us, or will buy from us hopefully real soon." I was actually shocked at that. It made me feel "sticky." I felt guilty being associated with a company that would rig a contest, not play fair, and cheat. Most of the people would not have filled out an information sheet, scanned their nametag, or even dropped their business card in the fish bowl, had they thought the contest was even the slightest bit rigged. I mean, why would you enter a contest if there were no chance to win?

I knew right then I didn't want to work with this company in the future. If they would do that, they would do other shifty things. Now I know some of you are thinking this is no big deal, everybody does things like this behind the scenes. Right? Well not everyone.

Do you feel in your heart and mind that just because most people do this sort of thing every day that it is okay? Consider this: If there are 100 flies in a room and

99 flies are stuck on the flypaper, and one fly is buzzing around the room, is the majority always right?? You may be the one doing the right thing.

I am not saying I haven't done anything unethical in my life. Believe me I am no goody-two-shoes. However, if you strive to be an honorable, honest human being, you will stay away from this sort of activity.

Our standards do not get lowered in one day. It is done gradually, one day, one hour, or even one minute at a time. Pretty soon, you don't even realize the person or company you have become. So raise your standards and live like a king that has high standards. Remember, what goes around comes around. You do the right thing, and good things will happen. People will treat you right. Why? Eventually, if you raise your standards, you will do business with people and businesses that have raised their own standards. Everybody wins. Oh believe me, the losers will seek each other out! If you happen to be a person or company that lives with high standards, as well as high integrity…good for you. Hey who knows, someday our paths might cross, I certainly hope so.

Magical Gem #14

Embrace integrity. When you raise your standards, the right people will follow you.

It is unreasonable to expect others to listen to your advice and ignore your example.

Movies And Real Life

(sometimes they are so close)

A really good friend of mine invited me to the movies. We'll call him Joe because that's his name. We went to see Pirates of the Caribbean. In my opinion, it's a great movie for anyone 13 years old or older. It was sort of a humorous ghost story. I won't blow the plot for you, but there was one scene where two pirates were each drinking a mug of rum. One of the pirates proposed a toast as they clinked mugs together. He said, "Don't forget the pirates creed – TAKE WHAT YOU CAN, AND GIVE NOTHING BACK" and then laughed. That was really sincere of them, as pirates, and true as well. The sad and unfortunate thing is, it is also true of many people today. That creed might be okay for the pirates, but I don't think it would be good for us. Not as individuals or the world as a whole. Let's talk…

If everyone thought like that, we as a people would be in trouble. Can you just imagine what that would be like? "Take what you can, and give nothing back!" I am not sure, but I think that's how wolverines eat with a "take what you can" attitude. I would hope the feeling you get would be empty.

On the other hand, the feeling you get from giving while expecting nothing in return is unparalleled. Many times, as the giver, we can be blessed as much as the one on the receiving end.

Let's take the second part, "give nothing back." Can you just imagine that? "Give nothing back." I'm not talking about reciprocating for a gift received. I am talking about giving nothing back to society. How empty.

I feel the human creed should be to help others as much as you possibly can. Or, Be willing to help anyone, anywhere, at anytime. This one single thought would elevate our society immeasurably. If you start giving back to society or even increase what you are already doing, you can and will make a difference. Your efforts will make a positive difference that can change our selfish world. It all starts with the person in the mirror. The world thanks you!! Thank you from a needy world desperate of more givers to share their time and gifts to the less fortunate.

Someday is no day, start giving today. When you come to the end of your journey, you will be glad you did!

Magical Gem #15

The reward you get from helping others may be unseen and limitless. Try it at least once and you will understand.

The Gift Of Forgiveness

One Sunday night I went to see and hear a speaker-evangelist who was addressing the topic of forgiveness. At the end of the program a man approached him and told him he had been feuding for thirty years with his neighbor over something having to do with finances. He gave his neighbor dirty looks, called him names, and pretty much hated the guy. Then after hearing the presentation, he decided he would finally forgive his neighbor. The man said to the evangelist, "Aren't you proud of me, I decided to forgive the guy after thirty years?" I think the man thought he would say, "Good for you," but instead the evangelist surprised him when he said, "It took you thirty years to forgive the guy? Are you telling me it took you thirty years of thinking about that issue? That's a long time for someone to rent space in your head. You lost time and effort on other productive things you could have been doing, and decided to cloud your mind and your heart? Well, I am glad you finally forgave the guy. Shame on you for waiting thirty years of your life to do it."

Don't ever lose thirty years of your life waiting to forgive. Do it as soon as you possibly can. You will save yourself lots of grief and heartache. That man thought he was going to receive positive accolades, but instead he received a little advice. The advice was…don't waste time and effort, forgive, forgive, forgive right away. Good advice.

Freedom Through Forgiveness

Over my lifetime several people have betrayed, deceived, or hurt me. Some owed me money; a family member took a huge advantage of other family members; an acquaintance wrecked my nice motorcycle and never paid me back; others lied, cheated, called me hurtful names, and even broke my confidentiality. All theses things hurt, and I mean a lot. I chose for years, like that man not to forgive. One of my favorite slogans then was, "I don't get mad. I get even." Wow, I learned by doing this that the people who wronged you win time and time again. Buddy Hackett once said, "While you are getting bent out of shape, the other guy is out dancing." How true. What a lesson I have found in the past. It is so-o-o-o-o-o hard for me to forgive. I am in a great mood 98% of the time, but when one of those specific situations would enter my mind I would get angry, losing out to the situation over and over again. Then one day someone said to me, "What if God, or even other people, forgave you like you forgive others?" I thought to myself, "Wow, I wouldn't like that too much." So I decided to get good at forgiving. We don't live in a vacuum. There will always undoubtedly be people who hurt us, but if we "allow" their actions to get to us, then we are the ones who will pay the price. Which translates into more stress and who needs more of that? We all know that stress over a prolonged period impacts our health. I would encourage you to forgive. It's a little over looked gem in life. It's one of those little secrets that not everyone gets to enjoy. The Bible says it well when it instructs us to forgive 7 times 70.

Forgiveness Continued…

Here's another story that demonstrates forgiveness in action. I went to see a friend from whom I had borrowed a large sum of money. When I approached him in his office I said, "I have to ask for your forgiveness." He said jokingly, "You didn't sleep with my wife did you?" We both laughed and I said, "No, but seriously…" He interrupted and said, "Scott, no matter what you ask to be forgiven for, you, my friend, are completely and totally forgiven. In fact, you are forgiven for everything you may ever do to me for the rest of my life. Now, what was it you think you have to be forgiven for?" I said, "I owe you money that I was supposed to pay a long time ago and am still unable to pay." He said, "You are forgiven completely. Pay me if and when you are ready. It's okay." What a reprieve he had given me. It was not paid back until over three years later. Thank you, Jeffery, for teaching me how I might forgive others the rest of my days.

Magical Gem #16

Just as we must love ourselves before we can love others, we must also be able to forgive ourselves before we can forgive others. The quicker this is done, the better it will be for all. I am still a work in progress. How do you forgive yourself? I haven't learned this one myself, yet.

Forget the past. What are you going to do now?

Untapped Potential

One time on a trip to Aruba I couldn't sleep. I was awake all night. At 6:30 am I decided to take a stroll on the beach to walk to the lighthouse. After walking on tons and tons of coral I stumbled upon a cactus growing between two pieces of coral. The cactus had conformed to the coral. Yes, a cactus seed had drifted some how into the coral. It was fine for a while, but as the cactus grew up it was confined to its surroundings. When just two or three inches away was plenty of room for it to grow to it's full potential. Isn't that just like us in a way? We drift into a situation and conform to the surrounding environment and stagnate. Fortunately we as humans have more options than the cactus. Sometimes just moving or doing something a little differently can remove us from a situation, allowing us to grow to our full potential.

Magical Gem #17

Explore your positive options to better your life. Usually there are more options than you think!

Fair, Just, And True

There is an old saying, "It's not the cards you are dealt. It's how you play the hand." No one ever said, "You know, life is really fair, everybody in life gets a fair shake" because this simply is not true. Life really isn't fair. Let's take, for instance, just being born in America. You are one of seventeen fortunate enough to be born in a free country. Is that fair to the person who starves to death in another country? Why are we the chosen ones? How about the person who dies from AIDS that got bad blood from a blood transfusion, etc? Is that just? The truth is that life is a gift. Each and every day should be treated as one. Instead, people take life for granted. People tend to bicker and complain about the smallest of things.

Gandhi once said, "If you want change in this world you must be that change." Things are not going to be fair. Everyone in life isn't dealt four aces or even a Royal Straight Flush. So what's the answer? You, the person in the mirror… you must make the best of it. You must adjust and change. You say this isn't the life you ordered, tell me about it. So it comes down to playing the hand you are dealt, right?

Let me give you an example. Gandhi was stepping onto a train that had just started moving when suddenly his foot got caught on the edge of the floor causing one of his sandals to fall onto the ground. He immediately took off his remaining sandal and threw it onto the ground next to the first one. When asked why he did that, he responded that one sandal was useless to anyone, but someone could benefit from a "pair" of sandals. What a cool philosophy! It was smart, thoughtful, and kind. How do you think most people would have handled that? They would have griped about losing that one sandal the whole train ride and would have told the story with one sandal left in their hand. Am I right?

Which would you do now that you know that story? Come on, admit; be honest. Mid way through my writing this book my mother developed lung cancer. After finding out the results of her test she immediately replied, "You know, I have been very blessed and fortunate most of my life to have very little pain." I am not kidding. It is true about the pain part. She broke her wrist one day and said, "it's okay, I have another one." She also said about the cancer, "I win either way. If I die, I get to be with my husband, Jerry. If I live, I get to watch my grandchildren grow-up." You just have to play the hand you are dealt to the very best of your ability. What's the alternative? Complain, complain, complain, equals stress, ulcers, etc. If you have no illness for a full year and one day you get the flu, are you going to complain you got the flu that year, or be very thankful for the three-hundred and something days you enjoyed being healthy as a horse?

Do you get my point? Be happy and thankful for what you do have, not what you don't. Don't compare yourself to others. There is always going to be someone stronger, faster, younger, and better looking than you. Yes, you heard me, better looking than you! Just concentrate on being the very best you can possibly be. That should be your never-ending goal. This isn't the life you ordered. However, it is the best one you could possibly hope for. This book will end, but fortunately it is only the beginning of your new life, your new attitude, and your new journey. Make the most of it. As John Swift said, "May you truly live the rest of your days!"

On your worst day you are somebody's best hope.

Financial Success Is Everything! Or Is It?

I was at a Speakers Association meeting. Where there was a man, an out-of-towner, talking about how successful he was, how many books he sells, and on and on about how much money he made last year, about how much he's making this year, etc. That was all he talked about. There is absolutely nothing wrong with sharing your success stories. But, he, however, was a bit excessive. To be honest, up to this point I hadn't said a word. At break time he invited me to join him walking to his car. He showed me his calendar to prove how booked up he was and asked me if I realized how much money that added up to. Then he told me, again. At this point I'd heard enough financial bragging and said, "Steve, it looks like you are making a lot of money, but is that all you ever talk about, the money end of it?" I asked, "Are you enjoying your journey?" He stopped, then with a puzzled look, paused a moment or two, looked back at me and to my amazement said, "No, I am not. I am at odds with my wife and I never have enough time with my children. I never stopped to look at it like that. Wow, thank you for making me realize that it's not just about the money." The journey may be even more important than the money. So whatever job you do, whatever success you have, stop yourself and ask, "Am I enjoying the journey?" If not, then make some necessary adjustments. You will be mighty glad you did. Who knows, if you are fortunate, you may even enjoy the journey as much as the destination.

Magical Gem #18

Money is not the be all end all. The riches come from enjoying your magical journey.

The best way for a person to have happy thoughts is to count their blessings and not their cash.

A Little Story

This is a story about four people named Everybody, Somebody, Anybody, and Nobody. There was an important job to be done and Everybody was sure that Somebody would do it. Anybody could have done it, but Nobody did it. Somebody got angry about that, because it was Everybody's job. Everybody thought Anybody could do it, but Nobody realized that Everybody wouldn't do it. It ended up that Everybody blamed Somebody when Nobody did what Anybody could have done!
- Author Unknown

Magical Gem #19

Step up to the plate and take the bull by the horns. Get involved, the rewards can be tremendous.

One of these days is none of these days.

Common Sense Isn't So Common

Every time I buy or discover a new prop for my comedy magic show I get so excited. I do an impression of a very famous magician that I refer to as "David Copperhead." He uses a lot of fans and smoke in his act. Oh by the way did I mention he uses a lot of smoke? As a parody to him I was looking for a product that would produce smoke that I could use in my act. I found an ad for a gimmick that stated the product was safe, non-toxic, non-hazardous, safe for the environment, and easy to do. At this point I must say that I do not feel that a magician/entertainer should ever endanger himself just for the sake of entertainment. For example being in a straight jacket suspended upside down from a cable that has been set on fire. I don't know about you, but that scares me! That being said, the smoke product I ordered came with all kinds of warnings about potential health hazards such as not to rub your eyes, don't get it in your mouth, don't breathe the fumes, and wash your hands immediately after every use. I could just see myself having to leave the stage to go wash my hands! I couldn't possibly do that because the hand dryer in the bathroom takes at least 4 – 8 minutes! Even though other performers may choose to use this gimmick, for me it was just not worth the risk. I can just imagine, years later growing a third arm or my hair falling out (faster than it already is) or even my ears falling off or growing a second head, or whatever. For me it was just common sense to pack it up and send it back. It was not worth the risk. My point is that people make so many goofy decisions in their life (including me). With some decisions, like this chemical thing, I think it's a no-brainer and could have far reaching consequences, but common sense is not so common. We should not make decisions based on fear, but the exact opposite. Educate yourself to the point that you can make better, more informed decisions. That makes good common sense, don't you agree?

Magical Gem #20

A t-shirt I once read said, "If you think education is expensive, try ignorance!" Common sense is just stopping and thinking through the situation. I know it's hard in the fast paced hustle bustle world of ours; however, slow down and think things through.

Reaching Out For Something Better

When I was a young boy living in Plymouth, MA, The Plymouth Rock was only a block away. How cool is that? We used to play on the ship, the Mayflower, okay, okay when security wasn't watching. We fished off the pier along with some others who were catching crabs. Some of the fishermen had buckets that were only eighteen inches tall that were full of crabs. I asked the fisherman if he was afraid that the crabs would get out of the bucket. He told me he wasn't because one of the other crabs would always pull the climbing crab back down. I would look into the buckets and watch them. Sometimes I would see that one of the crabs seemed to be sick and tired of its current situation. It would appear to want more than just what was being offered scurrying around and getting nowhere. The crab would reach for the top, begin to make some progress, and almost pull itself out of the bucket when another crab would reach up, grab the ambitious crab, and pull it back in with the others as if to say "welcome home!"

There are going to be people that will pull you down. Get away from those people. If you can't get away, learn to at least deal with it to the very best of your ability. If the "crabs" in your life are co-workers, try to change the situation into a positive one. If you keep trying and nothing seems to work, then you have no other choice but to avoid the people that pull you down. Don't give up on them completely because they could still change, miracles happen every day.

Magical Gem #21

Surround yourself with people and things that make you laugh and help you to grow even more positive. Never stop reaching for the top of the bucket, if you do, you will never find out what's on the other side.

The funny thing about life, if you refuse to accept anything but the best you very often get it.
-Somerset Maugham

Real Magic

One summer night a good friend of mine, Marshall and I pulled up to a stoplight. In front of us were five rough looking guys, long hair, and leather jackets. You get the picture. Marshall "Beeped" the horn to remind those guys that they could take a right on red. They looked around at us as if to say, "Don't do that again." My friend, amused with their reaction, leaned over and beeped again, "Beeeeeep!" It was as if they were bees in a jar, and we had just shaken the jar. These guys were mad. They were fuming. At this point, I was thinking roses would be nice at my funeral. Luckily the light turned green. Unfortunately, it was rush hour traffic moving bumper to bumper at a snail's pace. All of a sudden the guys turned into the first parking lot on the right. Three of the five guys jumped out of the car, put their fists in the air, and waved us over saying, "Come on! Come on" egging us on to fight. Little did I know I was about to learn an extremely valuable lesson as Marshall said, "I have their fate in my hands." I wasn't sure exactly what he meant until he leaned over and beeped again, "Beeeeep," this time adding a smile and a wave. Those guys went from fists in the air, to hands by their side, to smiling and waving back as if they just might know us. When people ask me if I believe in "real magic," I answer with a resounding "YES" as I think back on this story. I remind myself that you can change the outcome many times by changing your attitude. This little magical secret, if learned, will catapult you to a happier place that only a select few will ever know. When you can change someone's attitude at work, home, or anywhere with a smile, wow, that's real magic!!

M y
A ttitude
G reatly
I mproves
C ircumstances

Magical Gem #22

Wise people know the power behind a smile. It is as sharp as a double-edged sword; learn to use it to your advantage. A smile is like getting a face-lift for free.

Full Bloom

One day I gave my wife some roses. A few days later, they were all in full bloom, except for one. One, still in the form of a bud, had dropped off the stem and onto the floor. I picked it up and headed for the kitchen to throw it away. I wondered how many petals were in a rose, so I counted them. I discovered that the rose in bud form had the same amount of petals as the fully bloomed flower. The bud had the same potential. I was taken back on how parallel that is to our very own lives as human beings. It's tragic, but did you know that on an average day in the U.S. there are eighty-one suicides? Eighty-one suicides, you can't tell me that's not stress related. Just like the flower that decided to give up. My question to you today is...will you bloom in your lifetime? Some of us reading this book already have. Sure it may take some work. Just like the caterpillar works to become a beautiful butterfly. How many petals are within you? Two, four, six, or.........a thousand?

Magical Gem #23

Recognize the potential within us all. One of life's biggest disappointments is not what you did, but what you didn't do. That is a shame. Don't hold back, become the person you were meant to be.

The quality of a person's life is in direct proportion to their commitment to excellence, regardless of their chosen field of endeavor.
-Vincent T. Lombardi

Top 10 Suggested Books To Read To Make You A More Successful Person!

1. The Bible
(There's a lot of wisdom inside, no matter what your spiritual beliefs)

---

2. How to Win Friends and Influence People
Dale Carnegie

---

3. Seeds of Greatness
Dennis Waitley

---

4. The Magic of Thinking Big
Napoleon Hill

---

5. Miss Manners Guide for the Millennium
Judith Martin

---

6. The Book of Excellence
Byrd Baggett

---

7. The One Minute Manager
Kenneth Blanchard and Spencer Johnson

---

8. Sales Bible
(even if you don't think you are a salesperson)
Jeffrey Gitomer

---

9. Think and Grow Rich
Napoleon Hill

---

10. 14,000 Things to be Happy About
Barbara Ann Kipfer

Bonus Book
*This Book, the one you are reading right now!
Tell all your friends, thank you! LOL*

There are many more great books out there. These ten books changed my life to the better, period.

We grow by helping to develop each other's hearts and minds.

Teamwork In The Wild

A group of five of us were out on the golf course having fun, enjoying the sun and the friendship. John, my brother-in-law, was teeing off on the fifth hole of a par three golf course. He swung his club and hit his ball high in the air. Then tragedy struck, at least for one of the geese that was out on the green. John's ball hit a goose square on top of its head. We were all stunned, including the goose, which started to make a funny honking noise and wobbled badly as he walked. Then, an amazing thing happened. As the goose communicated to the other geese near him that he was in trouble, the other geese surrounded the hurt goose in a complete circle. They weren't even aware of what had happened to their comrade, but they were in support of him nonetheless. They encircled him protecting him, until he could get his bearings and start to walk normally. This took about three or four minutes and then the whole gaggle walked off together. We were in awe. As human beings, we could and should learn from this. If a situation arose at work or at home in which one of us were to get hurt or go through a tragedy, wouldn't it be wonderful if our fam-

Why didn't he just yell duck?

ily members, co-workers, and friends rallied around us with support until we got our bearings and got back on our feet? I would encourage this idea because someday, you never know where or when, you may be that very goose!

Magical Gem #24

Treat everyone with kindness. It may come back to you one day.

An eye for an eye makes the whole world blind.

Roadrage

(Letting It Go!)

On a summer day, almost twenty years ago my older brother Marc and I were riding in a pick-up truck on a major highway. Our windows were down and we were enjoying the breeze, not to mention each other's company. All of a sudden, out of nowhere, a man in a car pulled beside the truck and started yelling at the top of his lungs. He gave us sign language. I think he was telling us we were "number one." The man was yelling saying we cut him off blankety, blankety, blank. He was doing all of this at about fifty miles per hour. Our exit was quickly approaching. My brother said, "What is his problem?" My brother could have gotten all upset and retaliated yelling back and name calling along with sign language telling him he's number one also. But instead he chose to let it go and deal with the situation through humor. He looked over at me and said, "watch this." He then blew the guy a kiss and mouthed the words "I love you." The guy went nuts!! He got even more upset. As we took our exit my brother said, "Lets go get lunch." He was not upset in the least. Not many people would have handled that situation with humor, but it paid off. There is no telling how long that man was angry. I do know this: by my brother choosing to let it go, he benefited a lot more than that man did.

Magical Gem #25

Let it go. Don't get bent out of shape with the little things. Anger manages everything poorly.

You can't control others, you can control your reaction to others.

What's Best For Everyone Not Just You

My first adventure living on my own, moving out of my parent's house was exciting. I was thinking to myself, I could do anything I want. I never thought before I moved out about bills. Wait a minute these bills come EVERY month. Yikes!! One weekend my two roommates were each going to be away. Yes, I had the house to myself.

I invited my girlfriend and another friend over for a cookout. He asked, "What's that in the huge fish tank?" I answered, "Those are my roommates Venezuelan Rattle Snakes. He tells me they are ten times more venomous than regular rattlesnakes. The female is pregnant and he sells the baby snakes for $100 a piece. They usually have ten babies. That's some moola!" My visiting friend said, "Wow, that's cool" and then tapped on the glass. That startled the female and got her attention. He asked, "Do they ever rattle their tail?" I said, " Only if they sense danger and want to warn you to back off." Just then my friend tapped on the glass a second time. I said, "We better stop that, she's getting mad." He tapped a third time thinking that it was funny and that being behind the glass he was perfectly safe. The female was rattling away. My friend said, "That's cool

♦ This Isn't The Life I Ordered ♦

when she rattles." The female was so upset with the glass tapping and not being able to strike us that she turned to the male snake. She struck him right on the neck just behind his head. We jumped back three feet and were in shock. I know my friend did not want that to happen. My friend just wanted to make the snake rattle, that was all, period. I said, "That's just great." The male looked real sick, was acting very sluggish, and his head was dangling. I said, "My roommate is going to kill me when he gets home and I am going to have to buy him another snake." I had an idea. I called the pet shop and told them what happened. They said, "There's nothing you can do. He's either going to live or die, it just depends on him and his will to live." After three days of sweating it out thinking that he was going to die, the snake started acting normally again. My roommate returned, looked into the tank and said, "How are my babies doing?" He looked at me and said, "Thank you for looking after my babies." I didn't say anything because the male snake survived the bite and everything turned out okay. My friend and I should have known better, but we were only in our early twenties!! We shouldn't have been selfish just wanting to see the rattle go off. We should have known something was definitely wrong with teasing the snakes, not to mention the really dangerous situation we were in.

Magical Gem #26

It's best to consider everyone involved, and what would be best for all, before making decisions.

Why Complicate The Simple?

When my wife, Dede, and I bought our very first house together, we were really excited that we got pretty much what we wanted: cathedral ceilings, a large master bedroom, two bathrooms, and yes, a fireplace. The very first week Dede said, "Let's have a fire in our new fireplace." I tend to be almost too cautious and am considered too careful by all my friends and family. In fact one of my nicknames is "Mr. Safety." I said to my wife, "Let's wait and have a professional take a look at it first. I mean, we might burn a bird's nest or have a chimney fire from soot build up, or worst of all burn our new house down." So, we decided to wait.

During this time, my wife and I were on the road about seventy-percent of the time. When we were in town we would forget to have the chimney sweep check out the fireplace. When we were out of town, that's when we would think of it. Before you knew it, it was springtime. No need for a fireplace. But soon enough it was fireplace time again and we still did not think to have the chimney checked out while we were at home. Finally Dede and I were visiting her folk's house. They had a fire going. Dede said out loud for everyone to hear, "Boy, I wish we could have a fire like this at home." My father-in-law, Jack said, "Why can't you?" I said, "I want to have a professional chimney sweep look at it, but we never think of it when we are in town." He said, "Why don't you check it out yourself?" I said, "I don't know anything about fireplaces." He said, "Just open the flue and look up and see if anything is blocking the passage." I said, "That's it?" He said, "That's it. Just make sure there is no build up of creosote, either." I said, "Okay!" All this time I thought it would involve ladders, getting on the roof, flashlights, and soot all over the place. I didn't know. Well, I went home, opened the flue, looked up and it was clean as a whistle!! I can't believe we did not have a fire for a little over a year!!

You know, sometimes as human beings we complicate the simple. It is astounding how just a little information, or the right information, will diminish fear and worry, making a problem or situation become simple once again. "We should not fear the unknown. It is only to be understood." I have to go now. My Dede is calling me over to our soon to be rip-roaring, romantic fire in our clean as a whistle fireplace. Does anybody have any matches?

Magical Gem #27

Sometimes we make things more complicated than they need to be. Take the time to think it through.

Many of life's failures are people who did not realize how close they were to success when they gave up.
-Thomas Edison

Leadership Skills At It's Best

As we have discussed earlier, anger manages everything poorly. Anger is one letter short of danger and should be avoided like the plague. This story is just one of many fine examples of my Father, Wilbur G. Francis. In fact there were so many stories that my four brothers and I called them Willie-G-isms. It was 1979 and I was nineteen years old. My mom and dad wanted me to pick them up in the Winston-Salem, N.C. airport, a very small airport at that. The terminal is located on a hill. Ok, it is more like a dirt mound. I pulled into the parking lot at the bottom of the hill. I got a parking receipt and then realized I had pulled into the wrong place. I was supposed to pull up to the terminal to get my parents and not park at all. I made a u-turn and headed for the exit where you pay your parking ticket. There were two cars already in front of me that had to pay for their parking tickets, which took a total of two minutes. When it was my turn, I pulled up to the parking booth and said to the man in the booth, "I'm sorry I pulled into the parking lot by mistake. I was supposed to pull up at the terminal. I am only nineteen. I didn't know exactly where to pick up my parents and therefore made a mistake." The man in the booth, without saying a word to me, pointed to the sign below his sliding window. The sign read: 1 min. to 30 min.$1. He then put his hand out to collect the money. I said, "I made a mistake. Right when I pulled in I immediately made a u-turn to leave, but there were two cars blocking my way out. I could have pulled out of the parking lot in under twenty to thirty seconds tops, if it weren't for those cars." He again, not caring what I had to say, pointed at the sign and said, "It's a dollar." "But sir," I said, "I made a mistake and couldn't get out fast enough because of the two cars." He again stuck his hand out and said, "I don't care, and it's a dollar." Now, I am all for rules and playing by the book, but this was a little ridiculous, don't you think? I didn't have time to discuss at length the situation at hand. I made one final plea and said, "You really want me to pay for my mistake of pulling in the parking lot, turning right around immediately and exiting (the man saw the whole thing take place within fifty feet)." He kept his hand out as if to say yes. I reluctantly paid him the dollar and left. I pulled up the hill and picked up my mom and dad. I was mad and felt the guy took advantage of me and my youth. I told my dad what happened and explained to him that it's not the dollar, it's the principle. I also had a sneaky suspicion that he stuck the dollar in his own pocket although I don't know for sure. However, I do know I felt cheated out of a dollar. My dad apparently agreed, because he said, "Where is this guy?" I started to walk toward the booth. He followed me and just before we got to the booth my dad asked me if I had a pad of paper and a pen. I did and gave it to him. We approached the booth and knocked on the window. The man slid the window open and said, "Yeah, what do you want?" My father said, "Is it true my son told you he made a mistake pulling in the parking lot, turned immediately around and left, and you still charged him a dollar?" The man replied, "Yes, I did" and turned sideways and looked down at the floor in an attempt to ignore us. My father asked him, "What is your name?" Without looking up at us he uttered, "Ralph." My father repeated, "Okay, Ralph" and wrote it down. Then he said, "What's your last name, Ralph, and would you spell it for me, please?" Ralph said, "Why do you want my last name?" My father said, "I want the newspaper to spell you name correctly when they do a story on this." Ralph, still with his head down paused, a pregnant pause at that, sighed, and immediately hit the button on the register with force!! The drawer flew open, he grabbed a dollar, still not looking up and shoved the dollar toward us. My dad took the dollar, and thanked Ralph. End of story. No anger. No arguing. No fist fights. Just a little leadership skills mixed with a little common sense. It goes a long, long way.

Sometimes we just have to think about it – keep a positive attitude and follow through. Bottom line is getting results. That to me was brilliant. It was handled in under a minute. My dad knew just what to say. I was only nineteen years old, but I learned an extremely valuable lesson. There are a lot of ways that situation could have been handled. You just have to get a little creative, take the bull by the horns and lead. Lead people to do better and get results without getting mad. Ralph might have been frustrated, but hopefully he realized the error of his ways.

Magical Gem #28

Look at the problem… think of the solution… Execute, follow through, and make it happen!
Bottom line…get results!!!

A good test of people's character is their behavior when they are wrong.

Seven Steps In Knocking Out Problems

1. Define Problems – if you have to, break it down.
2. List Possible Obstacles
3. List Possible Solutions – no ideas are stupid.
4. Ask People for Help – if you need it.
5. Don't Procrastinate
6. Follow Through – make it happen.
7. Do It Now – get it done and move on.

Humor With A Purpose #2

Early in my career, I worked with a speaker that got paid many times more than I did to speak. I am not mad, but it was five times more!! Who's counting? We just happened to be on the same flight. He was returning home to Washington, D.C., and I was connecting to another flight in Washington. He was flying first class; I was in coach. His seat had a carpet bulkhead/wall in front of him. I was seated diagonally across the aisle from him in coach and I could see and hear him very well. We became friends on this gig and discovered that flying made both of us a little nervous. His solution was a drink to make the flight easier. I said I talk to people and use humor as my distraction.

After boarding the plane, my new friend said out loud so all the passengers in the immediate area could hear, "I would like very much to buy Mr. Francis a drink because I am in first class and can afford it." At the same time he put his feet on the wall in front of him he said, "And Mr. Francis is sitting diagonally behind me and can't afford much." The flight attendant approached me and asked if I was Mr. Francis. I told her I was and she said, "Mr. X would like to buy you a drink." I said, "No thank you, but would you tell Mr. X (loud enough for first class passengers to hear) you would think he, being in first class, would have some class and get his feet off the wall." She went over to him and repeated what I said. He replied to her, "Mr. Francis knows I have to sit like this because I have a wooden leg." She returned to me and relayed what he had said. I retorted, "You tell Mr. X he can unscrew his leg and put it under the seat like everyone else!!" The whole section got a big kick out of our conversation. Before we knew it, we had taken off and not even worried about that portion of our trip. A sense of humor used right serves us humans well!!

True happiness may be sought, thought, or caught, but never bought.
- Anonymous

Looking For Love In All The Right Expectations

When I was young and dumb, still single, and dating, I used to think about the girl of my dreams. I mean, after all I was a romantic, right?? Well, remember I said I was young and dumb? I would go into a disco. You heard me, a disco. For all you people less than thirty-five years of age, that's a dance nightclub. I thought I had it all figured out. Find the prettiest female (model material), and try to pick her up. Did I mention that I was young and dumb?? Here are some examples of how well that worked out: I would take a girl to dinner, leave to use the restroom, and return and find other men asking my date for her phone number, that would get old. Or how about the model I dated, that every time I looked at her she was looking in a mirror. I am not kidding. Or another one that dumped a drink on my lap because she though I was looking at another girl. Jealousy is not fun.

I decided to make a list of all the things I wanted and didn't want in a girlfriend or a spouse. I had a list of fifty things, yes fifty! Like I said, young and dumb. There's nothing wrong with having some expectations. Just don't go crazy with them or make them unattainable.

After years passed of not being successful, I asked a friend in her sixties to take a look at my list to determine if I was being too unrealistic. She said, "After reading your list, there is only one person that could fulfill it. I see no way around it, you will just have to marry Jesus Christ almighty!" I laughed out loud and asked her if my list was really that tough. I wondered if I was setting the bar way too high. So, I gave it more thought, and then I realized if I really were to get everything on that list, get my perfect spouse, it would be a mismatch because I wasn't perfect. I must have forgotten that part. I was much less than perfect. I set my expectations way too high. I started to reevaluate the situation and cut the list down from fifty to forty-eight. Just kidding! I thought, okay, okay, three things I must have to get married: must worship the same God as I, must have a sense of humor, and not be jealous. By making my expectations realistic, I became much happier. I prayed and asked God to help me and I found my girl.

Which brings us to the funny part of my story. Dede, who was at that time my girlfriend, and I went to a water park on our second date. We had fun, and then changed in separate quarters out of our bathing suits into shorts and t-shirts for the drive home. On the way home, we stopped at a restaurant. We noticed it was a little chilly inside. This on top of damp hair from the water park made us cold. Since a sense of humor was number two on my short list, I decided to see if she would play along with me. I pulled my arms inside my t-shirt. I didn't care how it looked. I was cold, but that made it look as if I had no arms. My girlfriend, Dede, pulled her arms inside her t-shirt making it look as if she had no arms, as well. Just then the waitress walked up, looked at me, then at Dede, and then at me again with a puzzled look. I said to our waitress, "As you can see, we don't have any arms and if it's at all possible that you could feed us, that would be great!" The waitress replied without missing a single beat, "That will cost you extra." Dede said, "That's fine. The money is in my left pocket" as she nudged her left hip toward the waitress. We all laughed BIG. I said this girl is the one for me!!

Two-and-a-half months later we were married. To the date of this book being published we have been together nearly fourteen years and are very much in love. When we have an occasional argument, her sense of humor kicks in. She says, "We know who's right. We know who's wrong, so lets just leave it like that!!!" Both of us walk away thinking we are right. Bravo Dede Francis, bravo! We agree to disagree and that's okay. A sense of humor comes in handy for a healthy relationship. I got what I wanted in a wife, a girl with a sense of humor that is not jealous and worships the same God that I do. The rest is icing on the cake.

My Father told me when I was about nineteen years old; one of the ways you can prove you are in love is to ask yourself this question. If a train was coming down the track as you were walking with your other half and there was only enough time to jump out of the way or to push your loved one out of the way, which would you choose? Let's just hope and pray it doesn't ever come to that. I would push, no, more like shove her real hard out of the way. Oh sure, the train would kill me, but I would get the last say in the relationship and that's okay by me!

Magical Gem #29

The higher your expectations, the lower your serenity. Revaluate your expectations and make them more realistic. It will make you much happier.

Next week there can't be any crisis, my schedule is already full.
-Henry A. Kissinger

An Almost Perfect Marriage

In thirty years I only saw my parents fight twice. I am talking only two times. When I tell people that my mom and dad hardly ever fought they say, "What is your dad? A pastor or something?" I just think their secret was true love with mutual respect and that they always put each other first.

I myself strive for a marriage like that and always will. However, my wife and I do disagree on some things and that's okay. For example she's cheap. Okay, frugal and I'm not. I'm all for, "Let me get dinner" while out with another couple. Or let me tip 22-30% when we go out to eat and we get fantastic service. We constantly disagree on tip percentages at restaurants. I say, "Okay, you're probably right about it" and walk away thinking I'm right, and she does the same. We laugh about it because she knows I am probably not going to change. I want to reward good service. If I get a cup of coffee and sit at a table with a friend for and hour and a half, I might leave a five-dollar bill. What am I supposed to leave? Fifteen percent? I would be embarrassed. Sometimes it's okay to agree to disagree. Some days I don't agree with myself.

My wife Dede and I are two different people who are not always going to think the same and that's all right by me. As the old saying goes: Would you rather be right or happy? I chose the latter!!

All being happy is, having a bad memory.
              -Lou Holts

Feeling Good

I learned this lesson early in my career. I used to perform strolling close-up magic for the patrons at the Grand Hyatt Hotel in downtown Winston Salem, NC. I was nineteen years old and didn't miss one Sunday brunch in six-and-a-half years. That's approximately three-hundred-and-thirty-eight days of entertainment. Let me ask you, the reader, a question. Do you think I was in a good mood every one of those days before I went to work? The answer is NO!! Sometimes I would even be in a blasé, complacent type of mood. I heard older folks mention, "Fake it till you make it." I thought, "Whatever!!" Then I tried it, and believe it or not this technique actually works! Eventually this effort got me more positive comment cards than the entire staff combined. It pays big dividends if you open your mind and apply this method. If you act happier, you really do feel happier. Abraham Lincoln once said, "Most folks are about as happy as they make up their minds to be."

Magical Gem #30

"Fake it till you make it." Once it becomes a habit, then good for you, because habits are hard to break.

The worst bankrupt in the world is the person who has lost his enthusiasm.
-H. W. Arnold

Peace Of Mind Is There For The Taking
(So What Are You Waiting For?)

One summer weekday morning at about 10:45 am my phone rang. I answered it, and it was my brother Todd from Columbus, Ohio on the other end of the line. "Hey Scott, what are you up to?" I said, "Oh I am just sitting here enjoying my breakfast, a bowl of cereal with a banana, apple juice, and watching and listening to the birds." He laughed out loud. I smiled and said, "What? What are you laughing at?" He said, "I had breakfast at 6:45 am. A rice cake in one hand a soda in the other driving to work at 70 mph." We both laughed out loud!!

You may have heard the saying: Stop and smell the roses. When I was really young I used to think, what a corny little phrase. Today it rings true in my life. Most of the time I make an effort to stop and enjoy life. In fact, here are just a few examples in my life as well as others that we can learn from.

I was shopping for sunglasses one day. I was in a hurry just spinning the display rack. I didn't realize that there was an elderly lady on the opposite side. I was in a rush to get some errands done. Here I was spinning away, round and round to see all the choices. Suddenly, I noticed the lady and said, "I'm sorry, I didn't see that you were looking too!" She said, "That's quite all right, take your time, look all you want to. As for me I don't rush anymore than I have to. You see, I used to hurry all the time…rush here…rush there, until I had a stroke and it changed my life." That one statement from her stopped me cold. It made me question how important it really was to get all my errands done that day. It wasn't really all that important and certainly not worth a stroke.

Now I am not saying to never rush again at all. I mean if a bull is chasing you, move and move fast!! I'm just saying it doesn't have to be go, go, go all the time. As human beings we set ourselves up like that. Most of us are so impatient. Some of us are waiting on the microwave for thirty seconds and we hover over it and say, "Come on, hurry up!" I remember the five o'clock rush hour. Everyday rushing home, I would get frustrated with traffic. One day it dawned on me…the library was on the way home. I would stop and read for about an hour-and-a-half, then drive home in a relaxed state of mind, when it only took about thirty-minutes. It was either bumper-to-bumper for one hour and fifteen minutes driving through rush hour, or waiting an hour and thirty minutes with only a thirty minute drive home in a happier and more relaxed frame of mind.

We owe it to ourselves to get the greatest joy out of every hour we spend. We need to change the way we look at things. You and I both know we benefit with less stress. Why add more stress to our lives? Why not reduce our stress and enjoy what life has to offer? Again we try to fit too much into a day. So take a moment. It's only but a moment to realize the benefits. With balance comes harmony and harmony, brings peace of mind. You can think clearer and have better ways to do things more efficiently and more productively. If your day at work includes the boss wanting you to get a lot done, then a clear headed and happy person will be more effective. When you are happy, you are like a well-oiled machine. Right? Take that moment and look for ways to reduce stress and get some balance.

For example, if you have an hour for lunch and it takes you five minutes to get to your car, ten minutes to fight traffic, twelve minutes waiting in line for food, ten minutes drive back, and five minutes to run back to the office, then you really just had eighteen minutes for lunch. A lunch that you probably didn't enjoy because you shoved it down your throat; which added more stress and less balance.

Okay, let's just take this one idea: you pack a lunch and have a nice little picnic on a blanket or a patch of grass somewhere near your work. I know this may sound stupid, but just try it. I know you are saying, "I don't always have time to pack a lunch." Okay, what if you split the duties? Let's say that on Monday and Wednesday your friend makes you lunch, then you make lunch for the friend on Tuesday and Thursday, and then you order pizza to be delivered to your office on Friday. There's nothing wrong with that. You can make every excuse in the world to not try new things or new ideas that would buy you more time, keeping you more balanced and happy. All I'm saying is to look for new ideas, and then try them; you'll be surprised what a little creativity can do.

I had a job one time that made me drive in rush hour at 8:00 am. So, I asked my boss if I could come in at 9:00 am and work one hour late and end at 6:00 pm instead of 5:00 pm. Believe it or not, he said yes. Plus, I missed rush hour at 5:00, they should really call it "slow hour." I am not saying this will work for everyone, I am saying try new things. It makes your life more exciting, and again, you are happier. So, stay balanced and aim for that peace of mind.

I went on vacation with my wife, Dede. Dede is a type "A" personality. We just got married and little did I know I was in for the shock of my life. I'm a very relaxed person most of the time. I was really working hard and needed a vacation. We decided to go to Disney World. The first day she set an alarm. Did I mention we were on vacation? Okay, so she set the alarm for 8 am. She said, "Yeah, I want to be the first ones in the park. At 8:15-8:30 we'll ride this, from 8:35-8:40 we'll ride that, and so on and so on. We put twenty-five pounds of excitement into a ten-pound bag. At the end of my vacation I was ready to go back to work. I'm more relaxed on my work scene.

We finally talked and I said, "Dede, I am a turtle and you are a rabbit. Please don't try to convert me. I am a turtle and that's all there is to it." The reality of it is, after almost fourteen years of marriage we kind of met in the middle. She's slowed down and I picked up a little. However, we found our balance, our harmony, and our peace of mind. With some thought you can too.

Magical Gem #31

Peace of mind takes a little work. We just have to learn to identify the chaos, and then make the necessary adjustments.

When nothing seems to help I go and look at a stonecutter hammering away at his rock perhaps a hundred times without as much as a crack showing in it. Yet at the hundred and first blow it will split in two, and I know it was not that blow that did it – but all that had gone before.
-Jacob Riis

♦ This Isn't The Life I Ordered ♦

Overcoming Some Of Life's Obstacles

One afternoon I had lunch with one of my newfound agents that books me gigs. We were in a buffet line, filled our trays with food, and moved down the line. We were approaching the end of the line at the register to pay. My friend looked at me and said, "Can you carry my tray?" I said, "No, you get your own tray." We were both in our late twenties, healthy, and could handle our own tray, or so I thought. He said, "No, I am serious, I need you to carry my tray of food. I have a condition called familiar tremor and I will shake all the food off my tray. Will you get my tray?" I said, "I am sorry. I didn't know you really needed my help." He said, "Didn't you notice me shaking a little?" I said, "I thought you just drank too much soda or coffee with caffeine." He told me he had had this condition since he was a young boy. Kids would make fun of him day after day, taunting him relentlessly. He said it would really hurt his feelings.

One day he thought to himself, if I can't beat them, I'll join them. He decided he would laugh with them. So when his classmates would say, "Look at Brent, he's shaking like an old man." He would turn to them and say, "Yeah, I bet I am the only guy in the school that can thread a sewing machine while it's still running!" The kids laughed and then he continued, "It's great at my house, when my mom would have shake and bake chicken I would help. He was the best there was. You see, Brent could have felt sorry for himself. He could have felt bad when kids teased him. One day he decided to accept himself for who he was and simply laugh with them. Once he did that, it was no longer fun for the kids to pick on him because he let all the air out of their balloons, so to speak. Brent took all their power away when he decided to join in the laughter. This technique is called "disarming." If Brent could do it why can't everyone? It's up to you.

Magical Gem #32

Use the "disarming" technique to neutralize criticism. Ignore negative brutal criticism. Don't let others hold you back. Believe in yourself and don't ever look back.

The secret of success is to be relentless with your commitment toward your purpose.
-Scott R. Francis

True To Yourself

At this time in my life I had been doing comedy-magic professionally for about twenty years. I had performed magic for a lot of movie stars, professional ball players, and VIP's. I was not at all star-struck. I just viewed celebrities as people, some more talented than others, who just happened to get their kisser on T.V. and became famous. That's my view of famous people. They are still just people. I told my brother-in-law, Jayme, I had to get ready for an after dinner show performance. He asked me who I was going to do the show for and I told him some NASCAR driver and pit crew. He asked who. I told him I thought his name was Dale Earnhardt. He said, "You're kidding!!" I said, "No. Why? Is he good?" He said, **"He just happens to be one of the best NASCAR drivers of all time."** I said, "Really?" He asked, "Is there any way you could get me an autograph?" Since I wasn't star-struck myself I said, "I really don't like doing that." He said, "Please!!" I reluctantly told him, "If an opportunity presents itself I will." He understood. I arrived at the dinner, did my magic, had some fun, and collected my check. I was ready to leave, but had gotten a little lost getting to the event. I asked Teresa Earnhardt, Dales wife, for some directions out of that area. She told me Dale knew that neck of the woods like the back of his hand. She yelled across the room, "Hey Dale, tell the magician, Great Scott, how to get to I-85." That put me one-on-one, face to face with the NASCAR legend, Dale Earnhardt. He gave me the directions. As he handed them to me I said, "Dale, I have a brother-in-law that's just crazy over you." He said with a grin, "You sure it's not you?" I smiled and said, "I really don't keep up with NASCAR. However, it would make my brother-in-law's year if I could get him an autograph, if you don't mind." "It's perfectly okay. if you don't want to." He said, "I'll give you one." As he pulled out his sharpie pen, he asked if I had some paper. I told him, "No, but being a magician I do have a playing card". As I fanned out my cards looking for one with a lot of blank space like an ace so he would have enough room to sign, Dale looked over and said, "Give me a three" (the number of his race car). I was thinking that I would give him a red three because the black ink autograph would show up better on a red card. I then passed him the three of hearts thinking to myself how clever, Dale Earn-"heart." He responded in a stern voice, "Boy, don't you know I am the intimidator?" as he threw down the red three. He said, "You get me a black three!!!" I started laughing and said, "Sorry, I didn't know you were known as the Intimidator." He signed the card and thanked me for the entertainment. I thanked him for the work and autograph for my brother-in-law. I was impressed at his view of himself. He didn't sway one way or another. He knew exactly who he was. Even in his heart and mind he was the intimidator. It would be a better world if everyone knew who and what they were. Their healthy view of themselves would probably take them further in life. If they focused and committed themselves to whom they really were. If Dale wasn't really sold on who he was, he wouldn't have cared what color the card was. Thanks, Dale, for being true to yourself to the end. You will sincerely be missed.

Magical Gem #33

Believe in who you are as a person. Stand firm and be true to yourself.

If you want to be loved, respected, and accepted then you love, respect, and accept yourself.

Looking Ahead

I love Pat McCormick's line, "tomorrow's a cancelled check." I love it because so many of us, including me at times, dwell on yesterday. "I can't believe what took place yesterday! I can't believe that happened to me" or "I can't take what she or he said or did to me last week" and on and on and on. Many people live with one foot in the mistakes and problems of yesterday and the other foot firmly planted in the "I cants," "what ifs," and "maybes" of today. Let it go, look to the future. The future is bright if you want it to be.

Is it me, or is aging a high price to pay for maturity? (Just a little food for thought.) Are you the type of person to walk into a grocery store, step up to the express lane, and count the items in the buggy in front of you? Do you get upset if there aren't twelve items or less? Forget about what you did yesterday. What are you doing today? You are what you practice most. So practice patience, humility, grace, and most importantly positive thinking. You have got to believe the best is yet to come to fully enjoy life.

I almost always have something to look forward

to. Remember when you were a kid and Christmas, a birthday, or some other special event would approach? Remember how exciting that was? Remember that feeling? Why does that have to change? Why can't we still have fun and look forward to things? Oh sure, the things we look forward to will be different than when we were a kid. However, there is still something in your life that excites you. You just have to figure out what that "something" is. I always look forward to a date with my wife. I always look forward to traveling, and yes I always enjoy returning home. I love to visit people, fly fish, play disc golf, and attend magic conventions. I look forward to what life has to offer. It makes living fun and interesting.

When I ask people what's going on in their life, if they have done anything exciting, or done any traveling, I hate that I usually get the same stock response. Most people reply, "Same old, same old." Well no wonder that boredom is one of the biggest reasons why people get a divorce. They get bored with each other. If you get bored with your girlfriend or your husband, or even with your very own life, do something about it. A speaker buddy of mine, Larry Winget, puts it this way, "If your life sucks, then you suck." Make your life interesting. Find out what drives your passion. Find out what blows wind into your sails. What makes you happy? If you figure the answer out, then who knows, you might even say, "I look forward to the challenging journey called life."

Magical Gem #34

Look forward with anticipation to life. Be open-minded and explore new hobbies, go new places, and meet new people. Life can be awesome if you allow it to be.

> *Life's not how long you live, but how well.*
> *-Kirk Douglas*

Good Communication A Must

I've always had a way with my wife, Dede, her way!! Good leaders know instinctively how to communicate. However; communication can be learned. I was going out to dinner with my lovely bride and we played out the typical scenario of most couples going out to eat. "Where would you like to eat tonight?" Dede replied, "I don't know. Where would you like to go?" I said, "How about Chinese," thinking she would probably go for that, since we haven't had it in a while. She agreed. So we ate Chinese food, finished our meal, and then she said to me, "You know, I wish we had eaten at the Greek restaurant." I said, "Why didn't you say something? I really didn't want Chinese tonight. I was just hungry and wanted to eat something. I assumed you'd go for Chinese. I really just wanted pizza." She said, "I would have gone for pizza." I didn't think she would like pizza, because she doesn't eat it that often. On the other hand, I eat pizza two or three times a week with no problem. Assuming she would most likely not go for pizza that night, I just suggested Chinese, thinking that would move things along.

This was an example of a typical lack of communication. I really could have had pizza. I was just trying to please her. She was trying to please me in agreeing to Chinese thinking that's what I really wanted. So, nobody got what they really wanted. I said, "Okay, let's promise to never let this scenario happen again."

This is what we do now and it works like magic. I remembered the technique that as a kid, my father taught us. He would say, "On a scale from 1 to 10, 1 being not very and 10 being starving, how hungry are you?" He would know exactly where everybody was, at that precise moment, and know whether to pull off the highway to feed his family, or to wait.

Now we apply the scale technique often and it works like a charm. I say, "I'd like to eat Italian. I feel like some Lasagna. On a scale of 1 to 10 how much would you like to eat there?" Dede might say, "I am like a three. How about you?" I might say, "I am an eight." She would say, "I could go for some Mexican food. I am like a ten for Mexican." I might say, "Okay, I'm like an eight for Mexican food." We decided to eat Mexican that night and were both pretty satisfied with the choice. Hence the problem is solved.

Other times she says, "I want to visit So and So on a scale of 1 to 10, where are you?" I might say, "I am a two on a scale of 1 to 10." She might say, "Is it alright if I visit this person myself?" We both end up happy with the decision. It works. It takes all the guessing out of trying to figure out where this person is, as we are not mind readers. This is an effective way to define your priorities and desires.

Magical Gem #35

Use this simple little one to ten scale method to greatly improve communication skills. <u>It works!</u>

Bound And Determined

This really is a humorous little story. To this day, every time I think of it I kind of laugh to myself. To think I got a life lesson at a company picnic. I was hired in my late twenties to do a magic show at a company picnic. It was a beautiful day, not a cloud in the sky. I did the show, and then it was time to eat. Everybody was excited that the food had finally arrived. There was fried chicken, barbeque, coleslaw, potato salad, and yes, corn on the cob. All the fixings of a good southern picnic. I saw lots of smiles, as people enjoyed themselves.

As I was observing the guests, I noticed a man with a big old smile who had only one front tooth. I am not making fun of him; but was just surprised when he reached for the corn-on-the-cob. Correct me if I am wrong in thinking that it would be nearly impossible to eat corn on the cob with one tooth. I was waiting and watching, without staring, of course. Then I said to myself, "Oh, he's probably going to whip out a pocket knife and shave the corn off the cob." Then I realized I was dead wrong. That guy started eating the corn on the cob just like everyone else did! Round and round he went. Oh sure, he was

♦ This Isn't The Life I Ordered ♦

missing a lot of the corn, and had to go around three or four times more than other people, but that didn't stop him. He was bound and determined to clean up! To my amazement he finished not only one, but two pieces of corn. I thought to myself, "Wow." This guy had very little tools to work with, but his determination to enjoy corn like everyone else shined right through. He stuck with it. He wasn't going to let the fact that he only had one tooth stop him. No way!!

It showed me that having determination can and will get the job done. I will tell you, I had no idea that day I was going to learn a lesson about determination at a picnic. I even used this little example to help encourage me when I was dragging in finishing this book. I remembered the man with determination and a belly full of corn.

Magical Gem #36

Be relentless in attaining what you are after. Keep on keeping on in whatever you pursue, undaunted with determination and you will succeed.

Do you hope to succeed or are you committed to success? It will show one way or another.

Raising Standards

Remember the old T.V. show from years ago called Melrose Place? There was an ad promoting the show that read, "Heat up your Monday nights, Melrose Place. Two-timers, back-stabbers, bed hoppers, is this great TV, or what?" Now don't get me wrong. All TV is not bad. I am just saying, be careful. If they can sell you a product in thirty seconds to a minute in a commercial, what do you think thirty to sixty minutes of exposure can do? You don't lower your standards overnight. It happens slowly. Before you know it, you're cooked. Stay with me for a minute. If you had a bucket and everyday you put red clay in it, at the end of the day you would have red clay, correct? Okay, if you fill up your bucket up with diamonds, what are you going to have at the end of the day? Well, for me I want my head filled with good stuff, gems if you will.

There was a man whose young kids asked if they could watch an "R" rated movie with only a little cussing in it. He said, "Sure you can if you eat some special brownies with just a little dog poop in it." The kids said, "No way, Dad." Then he said, "That's what you asked me to do with the movie with just a little dirt in it." That analogy made his point. How true it is! I know it's hard not to be exposed to some bad stuff, but work on raising your standards. I know it's easier said than done. In the movie, "A League of Their Own" a pro woman baseball player, played by Geena Davis is talking to the coach played by Tom Hanks about quitting. She said, "It just got too hard." And he replied, "It's supposed to be hard. If it wasn't hard everyone would do it. It's the hard that makes it great."

Feel good about yourself by making a positive contribution. I don't know about you, but I don't want to feel guilty about what I did yesterday. Guilt free is a great feeling. When you raise your standards, it raises your self-esteem, your outlook on life, and your quality of life. Try it for thirty days. If you don't see the benefits, you can have your misery refunded.

Magical Gem #37

Raise your standards and you will raise the quality of your life.

You become what you practice most. The choices you make today will impact you tomorrow.
                    -Anonymous

More On Expectations

My wife has a friend that she loves visiting and likes it when I go with her. But whenever I was there this woman's actions were totally out of control. She threw a chair across the room in response to something petty. I was really beside myself with her actions and struggling to accept her behavior. I must admit I wasn't sure what this lady was going through. However, her reactions seemed a little over the top. I do not enjoy visiting there because there is almost always some kind of incident.

One day while complaining to a friend about the abuse I experienced at every visit, the friend asked, "If a mentally retarded person kicked you in the shin, would you kick them back?" I said, "No, I wouldn't." He said, "Okay, what if the person you speak of is mentally or socially challenged?" I said, "I never looked at it that way. The truth is my expectations were not in line with this person's capability. She almost single handedly forced me to work it out in my life. I now realize setting high expectations of everyone will make me miserable the rest of my life. Expect nothing and you may be pleasantly surprised. When you get any positive back, be happy that you got any thing at all. I now view this person in a whole new light. I still don't feel really comfortable visiting there, and for now my wife visits a lot more than I, and that's okay. She accepts the fact that I am uncomfortable there and does not "expect" me to visit often. We now have an understanding that it is okay if I don't visit everyone she likes and I don't ask her to visit some people I like. I love my wife with all my being, and don't want to hurt her. We both just need to accept what we get. Now that we have learned to compromise our expectations and respect each other's wishes, life is so much happier.

Magical Gem #38

Expect less from people, and you will be a happier human.

Happiness??
A good cigar, a good meal,
a good cigar, and a good
woman – or a bad woman;
it depends on how much
happiness you can handle.
- George Burns

Seven Major Don'ts At Work And At Home:

Don't:

1. Gossip

2. Complain – If you have a problem, ninety percent of people don't care, and ten percent are glad you have the problem!

3. Be Jealous – It zaps your energy and confuses your focus.

4. Lie – Jim Rohm said liars lie because they are liars.

5. Take in too much negative – TV, Radio, or Newspaper

6. Admit you are wrong, EVER – or not take responsibility for your actions.

7. Always look for the bad in mankind. Lincoln said, "If you look for the bad in others you will certainly find it".

The Optimist Creed

Promise Yourself –
To be so strong that nothing can
disturb your peace of mind.
To talk health, happiness, and prosperity
to every person you meet.
To make all your friends feel that
there is something in them.
To look at the sunny side of everything
and make your optimism come true.
To think only of the best, to work only
for the best and expect only the best.
To be just as enthusiastic about the success
of others as you are about your own.
To forget the mistakes of the past and press on to
the greater achievements of the future.
To wear a cheerful countenance at all times and
give every living creature you meet a smile.
To give so much time to the improvement of
yourself that you have no time to criticize others.
To be too large for worry, too noble for anger,
too strong for fear, and too happy to permit the
presence of trouble.

Optimist International

Stand Up For Something You Believe In

One night, while I was returning from playing Disc Golf with a good friend visiting from Florida and one of the brothers, one of the guys mentioned that he was hungry and would like to get something to eat. He suggested hot wings. I said, "I would love to, but I had a date with my wife, Dede." They kind of kidded me saying, "Hey, if you're whipped, we understand." I said, " I am not whipped. I can go eat wings, but I made a promise to Dede a week ago that I would take her out on a date." In my mind I was thinking that I would like to go eat wings with the boys. Maybe I could postpone my date with Dede and make everybody happy. That was my first mistake, thinking I could make everybody happy. What was I thinking?

I called my wife and said, "Hey Dede, I am going to go get some wings with the guys. How about if we have a date tomorrow? I mean after all, my friend is leaving in the morning to go home to Fort Lauderdale. So, how about it?" Dede said, "Okay, but you promised me a date and I haven't seen you in a week." I replied, "Well, I'm tired and I think a date would be better tomorrow. Besides, my friend will be gone by then." With a sad voice she said, "Whatever you think is best." I said, "Okay, thanks babe." We hung up and I told the guys I could go, but I could tell I was disappointing my wife. They both said, "What? Is she guilting you into going with her?" At first I said, "Yeah, in a way, so okay, let's get some wings."

We stopped at my Mom's house where all our cars were parked. I said, "You know what, guys? I was thinking. I'm getting all wrapped up in this macho guy thing of doing whatever I want to do, instead of doing what is right." I looked at the guys and said, "I did make a promise a week ago that I would take Dede out on Wednesday night." I told the guys to go without me. "As for me, I am going to keep my promise to my wife." The guys said, "Okay, if you're whipped, you're whipped." I guess they thought that by using peer pressure, they could still get me to go with them. Believe me, it almost worked.

I thought for a moment and my conviction to do what was right prevailed. After the third or fourth time of being called "whipped" I said to them, "I have to live with this girl the rest of my life. Besides, I am taking advice from a bachelor and another guy that's on the brink of a divorce!" All three of us laughed out loud. Of course it's not true, my brother is not on the brink of a divorce. I just wanted to break their preoccupation with saying, "You're whipped, you're whipped, you're whipped." Once they realized the conviction of my decision, that I was going on a date with my wife, no matter what, they respected that choice and said, "That's cool.

You gotta do what you gotta do!" They left together and went out to get wings.

My wife was still out jogging, so I went inside to take a shower. I asked my mom to tell Dede when she came home that I changed my mind and we're going out on a date tonight. Mom said, "Okay." When Dede walked through the front door, saw me, and said; "I thought you were going to get wings with the guys." I said, "I was, until I realized the error of my ways. I did promise you a date tonight and I need to follow through and do the right thing. A promise is a promise. So, hurry up and get ready for our date." Her smile couldn't have been any bigger. I couldn't believe how happy that made her.

She took a quick shower and was about ten minutes from being ready, when she peeked around the corner with one of the biggest smiles I have ever seen on her face. I said, "What?" She said, "I feel like a million dollars. I know you wanted to go out with the guys, but you chose me instead! I feel like the most important human on Earth. Thank you so much for making me feel so special." I couldn't believe it. It's almost as though I just gave her diamond earrings or a brand new car. I was in shock that such a simple gesture made her feel that good. I know now I made the right decision. By the way, she buzzed for weeks about that.

It would have been easier just to go out with the boys, but I did make a promise. Getting wings was just a spur of the moment choice. <u>The bottom line of this story is that you are only as good as your word and that you have to stand up fore what you believe.</u> And I do. I believe in my marriage. I believe in promises. I believe in doing the right thing. Okay, most of the time.

By the way, it was a fantastic date. We had a blast. As for my friend, he ended up staying an extra day anyway. When you do the right thing, good things happen.

Magical Gem #39

Don't let your decisions be dictated by peer pressure. Be firm in what you believe. Stand your ground. It is noble to keep a promise.

People may doubt what you say, but they will believe what you do.

Attitude

The longer I live, the more I realize the impact of attitude on life. Attitude, to me, is more important than facts. It is more important than the past, than education, than money, than circumstances, than failures, than successes, than what other people think or say or do. It is more important than appearances, giftedness or skill. It will make or break a company…a church…a home. The remarkable thing is we have a choice every day regarding the attitude we will embrace for that day. We cannot change our past…we cannot change the fact that people will act in a certain way. We cannot change the inevitable. The only thing we can do is play on the one string we have, and that is our attitude…I am convinced that life is 10% what happens to me and 90% how I react to it. And so it is with you… we are in charge of our attitudes.

Chuck Swindoll

Peer Pressure

(Give Me a Break)

In the 11th grade I had to go to summer school at night to make up my grades. I was seventeen years old and believe it or not I would walk three-and-a-half miles to school and three-and-a-half miles back. I desperately wanted my High School diploma. I was bound and determined to get it. I was the youngest student in this class. The other students were between twenty-one and twenty-five years old. The teacher would allow us to take a ten-minute break from time to time. We would go outside and some of the students would smoke. The conversation would go something like this: "What's your favorite drink and snack?" One of the guys would respond, "Beer and potato chips." The next guy would say, "Beer and tortilla chips." All eleven of them mentioned a certain beer and a certain kind of chip that would go with the beer. It was now my turn. I said, "Milk and cookies." Everybody burst out laughing at my answer.

I told my dad the story and he said, "Eleven guys said what kind of beer they like with what kind of chip and you said milk and cookies? Wow, you didn't feel any pressure to say beer and chips?" I said, "No, why? I just told them the truth, that was what I liked." He said, "It didn't make you feel embarrassed?" I said, "No, not at all. If I had said beer and chips at the time I would have been lying." Besides, I would be living my life for them. The only one I live for is my Maker and myself. That's it.

Don't fall in to this trap. It can even happen long after high school. If you asked me to live to please mankind, that would be a big mistake, because I don't want to live up to everybody's expectations.

Magical Gem #39

Peer pressure is hogwash. Don't live your life to please man; it would be kind of like a prison for your mind. If you are doing your personal best, that is what counts. It was Madonna, no wait, Shakespeare that said it best, "To thine own self be true."

The man who cannot believe in himself cannot believe in anything else.
-Roy L. Smith

Low Self-Esteem

In our cynical world today, it is so easy to have low self-esteem. In fact, there are so many people with low self-esteem; we could call it an epidemic. A great many people cut down others to boost their own self-esteem. Instead they end up lowering the esteem of the person they are berating as well as their own. No one is immune from these people. It is up to us to not allow these people to get to us. It's like kryptonite to Superman. Ever notice how it is the only thing that gets to the super-hero?

I had a severe case of Dyslexia; I still do to a degree. I had to choose to overcome and not allow it to bother me. In school kids would make fun of me because I took a special class in middle school. There were only seven to ten kids in the class. We would get special one on one attention to help us with our learning disability. The kids in the normal classes would call me stupid or retarded in the halls. (Gee, I wonder how many of them wrote a book? I'm sorry; did I say that out loud?) I allowed them to make me feel stupid because of my poor reading skills.

Today I read no less than two hours a day on interesting subjects such as humor, magic, fly fishing, chess, personal development, etc. I do this because I know that knowledge is power. Knowledge is the next-door neighbor to success. It increases my self-esteem. Make the decision to choose activities that are in harmony with your values. When you allow other's opinions to get to you, you give them power over you. My friend Marge told me about a book entitled "What you think of me is none of my business" It made me laugh out loud. Let me just say that some people are going to judge you no matter what you do or say, even if you were perfect. That's just how they are. So, just keep on keeping on. Don't waste precious time dwelling on the past. Don't allow yourself to feel stupid. Learn from your mistakes, and then move on. Build your self-esteem by respecting yourself and what you do. Learn a skill. Improve your self-worth. Feel good about yourself. In my case I felt stupid, so I would read a lot. Finally one day, instead of feeling stupid, I felt quite the opposite. I might joke and say to people that I spell dog c-a-t, but I certainly feel good about my overall intelligence. In fact, I can't even watch TV without turning the brightness up. All kidding aside, life is way too short not to feel good about yourself.

When I was about nineteen years old, I joined a multi-level marketing organization that had a lot of positive people. I participated for about eight months. At that time I was fired up about building a business for myself. One of the achievement levels was called "Diamond."

People would cheer, "Go Diamond!!" That's what I wanted to achieve, the diamond level. I got so excited about it that I went home and wrote it in permanent marker in HUGE letters on my bedroom wall "Go Die mod!" That was a big joke for a long time in my very own home. For years and years friends and even family members would make fun of me. I would feel stupid and low about myself. Today, it doesn't even matter to me. It's not that important to spell perfectly to have success. What really matters? I have the job I love; a wife I adore, I make great money with lots of free time for myself, and I continue to get closer to God. What more could a human being want? For those still struggling with people in your life who make fun of you, remember it really doesn't matter what they say. What matters is how you feel about you. That is the bottom line. You can overcome and succeed if you choose to rise to the occasion. Only you can define your success and raise your self-esteem. Don't ever forget it. Choose to feel great about yourself. Who knows, someday you might even, "Go Die mod!" Whatever "Die mod" is to you! As for me "Diamond" or "Die mod" is about me feeling good about myself. That's what matters most of all.

Magical Gem #40

Raise your self-esteem. Don't let people and life pull you down. Do good things that make you feel good about you.

People who fly into a rage often make a bad landing.

The Big Rescue

Homer Simpson once said, "Does anyone know the number of 9-1-1?"

When I was about fifteen years old my brothers and I had a couple of gerbils. One got out of its cage and was missing for several days. Finally, a clue popped up. My mom and dad were downstairs in their bedroom when they heard a scratching sound coming from the wall, "Scratch, scratch, scratch"

They told us that the missing gerbil had apparently made his way into the wall of their bedroom. We thought about the problem, went upstairs, and stepped into the closet with flashlights. We approached the back of the closet, shined the flashlight between the 2x4 stud and looked down. "Voila." There was the refugee gerbil in plain sight.

Unfortunately, we lived in a house that had what is known as balloon framing. This made the wall studs even longer. It was approximately a twelve foot drop straight down. The area between the studs was only fourteen inches wide by four inches deep. Because this was an older house there was no insulation in this area

♦ This Isn't The Life I Ordered ♦

between the inner and outer wall. The fall to the bottom must have really hurt the gerbil.

We were trying to figure out a way to rescue the gerbil. One choice was to go downstairs and cut a hole in the wall with a circular saw. We knew we would wreck the wall and possibly hurt or even kill our furry little friend. We had to be creative. We could drop him a rope, but I don't think he would know to hold on……..hmmm. We had to really think. This was a serious challenge.

Then I got an idea. One of my brothers had a G.I. Joe Rescue Ranger set from when he was younger. We decided to give it a try. We tied a string on a fruit basket looking apparatus that would normally be used to rescue a hurt and wounded G.I. Joe.

The plan was to lower the rescue kit down to the bottom level. Then hopefully the gerbil would hop on the basket and we could all go home. Oh, wait, we were home. Unfortunately, the gerbil never would hop on the rescue basket. He ran around and around it, but never on it. We knew the gerbil had to stay on it in order to be pulled up to safety. Figuring he hadn't eaten in days, we decided to put food and water in the rescue basket. The gerbil hopped in the basket long enough for us to pull him to safety. "YEAH!" The excitement level was really high with the brothers. We were very happy it all turned out in the end. I mean……even a gerbil knows when to be rescued. There are people that don't know to ask for help. Who knows? Maybe you could lure them with a donut?

Magical Gem #41

If you need help, ask for it. Don't get frustrated. As we all know, you gotta A-S-K to G-E-T.

The world is moving so fast these days that the man who says it can't be done is generally interrupted by someone doing it.
-Harry Emerson Fosdick

Seven Questions To Ask Yourself:

Do you take time to reflect?

#1. What makes me truly happy?

#2. What activities give me the most satisfaction and inner peace?

#3. What are my three most important goals?

#4. What goals can I make happen now?

#5. What can I do that will make a difference at work or home?

#6. What, old friend, hobby, or activity have I forgotten about that I used to enjoy?

#7. What is my purpose in life?

Good Vibrations

Learn these simple rules and you will go farther than you ever imagined.

<u>When you smile</u>, it tells others that they are all right. This makes them feel good about themselves. It's communicates acceptance.

<u>When you listen</u>, you are really saying to the other person that they are important and that you care and value them.

<u>When you are sincere</u>, people can really sense that.

Be authentic, people can see through fake people like cellophane.

People are smarter than you think.

Reach out and go that extra mile with people and you will be liked and loved more, guaranteed. Apply this to your situation and it will bring you to a higher plane enhancing your very own life. These ideas may seem basic I know, but sometimes we forget the basics. We get too caught up in our busy lives to pay attention to the little things that make a big difference. So grab some good vibrations and enjoy your more abundant life.

The Magic Of Team Work

I bought this t-shirt that made me laugh, it said, "I deserve all the credit." Everybody knows at least one person like this. What does it matter who gets the credit? The bottom line is that the task gets done. Right? Don't you think what matters is that you know you did your personal best and that your efforts boosted that of your teammates? It really stinks when everybody doesn't pull his or her own weight, but that's life. What's important is that you deliver.

A magician I once met witnessed another performer on stage and commented, "He has this trick and that illusion, but I have this certain trick." I said, "Stop comparing yourself with others. Just look at the guy in the mirror and worry about if he's doing good. That's what really counts." Don't ever compare with teammates; just contribute your part to the best of your ability.

I don't remember who said it, but I love this saying; "I wonder how much we would get done if we didn't care who got the credit?" Encourage teammates to be the very best that they can be and watch what happens. It's more fun when everybody has one common goal, something to aim and shoot for. When you win, let everybody hold the trophy. Let everyone win, its more fun and more interesting.

I was watching a TV program about a maximum-security prison that held one hundred criminally insane inmates. It only took three guards to watch over one hundred prisoners. The interviewer asked one of the guards, "Aren't you afraid they might revolt?" The guard said, "Not really because <u>lunatics never unite!</u>" Wow! That's a powerful statement. If you want to accomplish great things, teamwork is where it's at.

Magical Gem #43

The best way to get involved is to get involved. It gives you a great feeling when you can truly share in the victory. Teamwork divides the effort and multiplies the victory.

Big people are always giving someone credit and taking blame. Little people are always seeking credit and giving blame.
-Charles Jones

How To Get More Time For Yourself

We all have twenty-four hours in a day, seven days in a week, and three hundred and sixty five short days in a year. Did you ever notice that some people seem to have a lot more free time than you? This is the magical secret of a chosen few. Come closer and listen.

Life changes when we change. If you want things to be different you must do things differently. For instance my wife, Dede, and I have been married for nearly fourteen years. When life gets hectic and chaotic sometimes, with friends calling wanting us to do things, or we are asked to volunteer for something or… Whatever makes it crazy at home, if we make it a priority to carve out a time that we can have a date at least once a week. We have it set up at our house with no phones (turn off the ringer and promise not to answer it) and no friends, just me and her, all to ourselves. We love it. You heard me! After fourteen years we have to make it a priority or it wouldn't happen. If you make everything important, then nothing is important. I love that time we have to ourselves.

Another priority I have is Disc Golf at least once or twice a week. That is exercise for me. It's approximately two-and-a-half miles of walking and throwing a Frisbee. That is time to myself. It's not only something that I want to do, but need to do as well. My wife knows that it is good for my health and makes me happy. She used to make me feel guilty for taking time away from business during the day, and playing all the time until I explained how important it was to me to have this time to relax and think. Today I don't feel guilty at all. It's okay to exercise. It's okay to notch out time for yourself, as long as there is a balance between your core values your and priorities.

Take the gift of peace of mind and take time for yourself. No matter how hectic things get, you need to step away from life's chaos for your health. You have to make time and just know you can't do everything. You decide what's most important to you, and then decide where you will carve out time for you. This is a must and beneficial to your well being. If you view it in that way, you will get your very own slot of time. Again, <u>if you make it a top priority, it will happen.</u> Take your slice, your very own chunk of time. I know you are probably saying, "This guy doesn't know my schedule." Believe me there are slots, nooks, and crannies. You just have to look hard enough and set your priorities. There's a good book that says, "if you seek you will find." So what are you waiting for? Seek!!!

Magical Gem #44

Set priorities and make time for yourself. You are worth it.

To gain extra time in your life is to definitely learn the word, *(say it with me,)* **"No!"**

Welcome To America

Don't get me wrong, I know we have problems. When I hear people complain about America, I have to roll my eyes. I hear them say we pay too many taxes, crime is high, gas is too much, yadda, yadda, yadda.

First of all, I want to challenge these same people. I want to tell them, yes, you could say gas is high. Okay, so move to a neighborhood where you can walk to your job and the grocery store, hook-up with a friend and car-pool, or use public transportation. These are all possible solutions. Next they say crime is high. Okay, be pro-active and start a neighborhood watch program. They say, taxes are too high. I say, I want to pay more taxes. In fact my goal is to pay more taxes than anybody I know. Why? Because it just means that I made more money. You can choose to look at everything in a different light. Complaining about things just pulls you down, as well as others and our country.

Be glad you live in America. I love America. I have been to other countries. Our standard of living is one of the highest the world has ever seen. When I see how others live in other countries, and then come home to the States, I realize we live like kings and queens and I never want to forget that.

We have cars. In other countries even the kings don't have wheels. We get to choose what we eat, not if we will eat. Our pets even have a whole aisle dedicated to them in the grocery store with different food choices. I love America. I always have, since day one, and I always will.

Americans are one out of seventeen people born who live in a free country. Freedom alone is worth the price of admission. It's not perfect. Nothing is. But love your country. Don't bad mouth it. If you have a problem with something, provide the solution. We need to show that we are united, not divided. As for me, I am proud to live in one of the greatest countries of all time. These people that make the decision to still complain can leave anytime! Have a good flight!

Magical Gem #45

Change how you view things. Choose to get happy and you too might say, welcome to the country I love. Welcome to America.

If you could kick the person most responsible for most of your troubles, you wouldn't be able to sit down for six months.

Customer Service?

(I Never Heard of Such a Thing)

A friend of mine asked if I would help him deliver a car. The plan was for us each to drive from North Carolina to Washington, D.C. Then, we would drop off the car that he had sold, and ride back together. I agreed to help him out.

I had grown up and lived in the Northeast, in Massachusetts for the majority of my life. Just ten short years ago at that time I moved to the southeast. One of the things I learned to enjoy in North Carolina was a sausage biscuit in the morning.

During the trip to D.C., I went to a very popular fast food chain and asked for a sausage biscuit. They said, "We don't carry those." I thought sausage biscuits were popular everywhere. The girl at the fast food restaurant said, "Why don't you try the truck stop across the street?" I said, "Okay, I will. Thanks for the tip."

I walked into the truck stop and said to the waitress, "Hi, could I get a sausage biscuit to go?" She said, "We don't sell sausage biscuits." I said, "You don't sell sausage?" She replied, "Yes, we do." I said, "Do you sell biscuits?" She said, "Yes, we do." I said, "I don't get it.

What's the problem?" I am not kidding you when I tell you she said, "Well, we sell sausage and we sell biscuits, but we don't sell sausage biscuits." I was dumbfounded!! I said, "Well can you sell me a biscuit, and then sell me a sausage, and I'll just put them together myself?" She said, "Yeah. We can do that."

I cannot believe she just didn't think of that solution on her own. In her mind it was complicated because it involved two different purchases. In my mind I was thinking about how hungry I was and that I felt like having a sausage biscuit. She couldn't put those together in her thought process. It boils down to this: if at all possible, just give the customer what they want and you'll make your customers happy. It's not that hard.

Magical Gem #46

A. Really listen to what the customer is asking for or saying.

B. Think outside of the box.

C. Deliver big.

Your Optimum Life

(Okay, here's what it takes.)

After listening to over two thousand cassette tapes, reading hundreds of books, and having literally studied success for twenty-five years, I have come to this conclusion. In order to feel good about ourselves, we have to strive to do better, continue to grow, and improve our lives. All it takes is pure determination.

Take a good look at a single brick. Ask yourself how many things could be done with that one brick. For example, it could be used in a negative way. Such as smashing in a car window, hitting a person, or even breaking a windowpane. On the other hand, it could be used in a positive manner. It could be used to build a beautiful brick home, to border a garden, or to build a patio. You see there are countless uses for a brick, wouldn't you agree?

Now let's consider that your life could be the brick. You can use it in a negative or a positive way. It's a tough decision to make. The secret is to know what you really want before you move forward. Once you take that plunge of knowing what you want, then desire has to follow. You would be surprised to know that I have talked to fifty and sixty year olds that still don't know what they want.

One summer, my brother, Kirk, and I were playing catch with a baseball. He was about nine and I was around eleven years old. We were throwing across an inlet of water that was four feet deep near the bank. We were doing pretty well for about thirty minutes. On my next throw I threw the ball a little short. It started dropping right over the water. To my surprise, Kirk, the athlete of the family, took off running and dove for the ball. He caught it in mid-air. He smiled and shrieked, "I got it!!" and then fell into the water.

I was shocked. I asked him, "Why did you decide to do that and get wet? Why didn't you just let the ball fall in the water, and we could get it later?" He answered, "I had to prove to myself that I could do it." I said, "I would have let that one go."

That was why he was so good at sports. He found the secret to success. It was desire. You've got to have desire. You have got to want it bad enough. Take these three steps:

#1 – <u>Decide what you want</u>.

#2 - <u>Have a desire.</u>

#3 - <u>Mix this with unstoppable determination.</u>

Then you will have discovered a formula for your personal best.

Don't give up. Don't ever give up. I am a dyslexic person that got C's and D's in school, but I never would have written this book if I didn't have desire and determination. No Way!! It wouldn't have happened. Take control of your life. It's your life, don't just wait for success to find you, make it happen.

Use this book to remind you to set up your launching pad for your successful life. Whatever that is to you. Ask yourself if your life is getting better today than it was yesterday. If you can't answer that with a resounding YES, then change a few things. Get on target and follow through. Do you hope for success? Or are you committed to success?

I heard a preacher say, "There are a lot of granola bars out there, a bunch of fruits and nuts." It's funny, but true. Don't let any fruitcake pull you down. If you decide happy days are here again, then, happy days are here again!

Magical Gem #47

A few years ago, I walked on a glacier in Alaska. It was really cool. The person I was with said, "Did you know that a glacier is always moving forward? It moves at a slow pace, but it continues to move." We should strive to be like that glacier and continue for the rest of our lives to always move forward.

Sleep – How To Get It

Experts agree that the one single thing you can do to drastically improve your life in one swoop is to get more sleep. It is estimated that in the U.S. at least forty percent of Americans don't get enough.

Did you ever notice that you feel great after sleeping six hours? However, if you take an extra thirty minutes then you feel kind of sluggish. Most people have no clue on how to sleep. I read about sleeping in cycles. This method works best if you try to schedule your sleep around ninety minute cycles. For instance, you should sleep one and a half, three, four and a half, six, seven and a half, or nine hours. If you break these cycles, then you will find that it is harder to wake up. It also explains why many people are sluggish after sleeping. The report says that seven and a half hours is the best amount of time to sleep for most people. However, you may feel better with six or nine. It depends on you and your activities during the day.

If I am dragging during the day I know I need a cat-nap. It makes me feel and function better. I usually take a twenty-minute power nap and feel great. If I take an hour nap I feel worse than if I had not slept at all. Experiment and find a formula that works best for you.

Everybody benefits when you improve your sleep habits. You will have more energy and add balance to your life. You will be healthier, happier, and less dangerous. You heard me, less dangerous. There are over ten thousand car accidents per day in the U.S. Could lack of sleep be contributing to the problem? My search for answers to my own questions about sleep made me the resident sleep, or lack of, expert among my friends.

Lack of sleep makes cowards of us all
-Vince Lombardi

Yadda, Yadda, Yadda

There once was a monk that lived in a monastery located on a cliff on the side of a mountain. The rule at the monastery was this; the monk could only say two words every ten years and had to take a vow of silence for the rest of the time.

It just happened to be the tenth year where the monk got to speak his mind. He stepped right up to the edge of the cliff. All the village people gathered down below in anticipation of what the monk might say. Then the monk spoke and said, "<u>Cold food</u>." The villagers were kind of baffled by his words having expected something more profound.

After another ten long years passed the same thing happened. The monk walked to the edge of the cliff. The villagers gathered below anxious to see what he would say this time. The monk said, "<u>Hard bed</u>." Once again the people were shocked and baffled at his words.

The head of the monastery came up to the monk and told him, "You have to leave." The monk asked, "why?" The leader replied, "Ever since you've been here you've done nothing but complain!"

This is a humorous joke that also has a strong message. Think about it. The monk had four words he could speak and they were all, one-hundred percent, negative. People in the real world don't want to hear complaints. I'll go as far as to say that ninety percent don't want to hear the complaining and ten percent are glad you have the problem.

All kidding aside, it's far easier to fall into a pattern of complaining. We all have gripes, aches, and pains and are tired, etc., etc. There are tons of things we could complain about. The challenge is to not fall in the trap of chronic complaining. It's so easy to do. It just pulls everybody down. It lowers the morale.

When I think of my problems, aches, and pains I think there is always someone else worse off than me. This makes me feel fortunate and blessed. I try to lift people up and not pull anyone down. I do my best to stay positive and fun. What is the alternative? Doom and gloom where nobody, and I mean nobody, wins.

I choose to think happy. I know it sounds ridiculous, but all that being happy is, is filling your mind with happy thoughts. That's it. That's the big secret. Choose to be happy, not sad. Choose to be motivated. Choose to have a great attitude. Choose to do all these things and you will have chosen a better life and will be the happy human, period.

If your life stinks, look at how you view things. Are you complaining all the time? If you are, you are going to talk yourself right into unhappiness.

Magical Gem #48

Choose to not complain. Choose to fill your mind with happy thoughts. If you are committed to choosing the positive path, you will go far.

Every minute you are angry you lose 60 seconds of happiness.

Caring Speaks Volumes

I was visiting a fast food joint. I'm not going to mention which one because the restaurant isn't the one I have a "beef" with. No bun, oops, I mean no pun intended. My problem was with the uncaring person behind the counter.

The restaurant wasn't busy at all. I asked for a plain cheeseburger. I just wanted cheese and meat only. The guy behind the counter looked right at me and said, "Do you want cheese on that cheeseburger?" My initial thought was to jump over the counter and thump him on the forehead. Correct me if I'm wrong, but I think cheese still comes on a cheeseburger.

I was really hungry and didn't feel like dealing with this person that wasn't listening to me, the customer. I looked at my friend, Morty, and he smiled. He knew I didn't have a lot of sleep and was finding it difficult to deal with this person in a civilized manner. He said to me, "I'll handle it, you go sit down."

I am so glad my really positive friend was there that day. We finished our lunch then I started to complain, "Can you believe that guy? I asked for a plain cheeseburger, just cheese and meat only and he asked if I want cheese on the cheeseburger." My friend, at my weak moment of complaining said, "You don't want to go there." I said, "What do you mean?" He said, "You don't want to go to that world." I said, "What world?" He replied, "The world of complaining and griping. Let it go. You're tired. Let it go. Come back to your world where you are happy again." I snapped out of it and thought to myself, that yes, I was being sucked into the negative world. It is so natural to do. So, I stopped, thought about it, and returned to my happy world. I thought that is such a cool way to put it. My friend uses the terminology of going into another world. We laugh about it often and remind each other not to go there, not into that world. What a great way to phrase it, thanks Morty for the gift.

As for the guy not listening to the customer, I can only change myself. If that guy doesn't want to listen and maybe never gets a raise or advances at his job, that's his deal. You could even say it's his world. Though, if he did choose to listen and care, he might have grown in his job and possibly have advanced. It is so easy to become a super star in customer service these days because it is so rarely done. Nowadays anyone can shine big time with just a minimum amount of effort.

Magical Gem #49

You have probably heard this before, but it's still great to be reminded. People don't care how much you know until they know how much you care. Genuinely care more about people and the response will be astounding.

Reputation And Character

The circumstances amid which you live determine your reputation; the truth you believe determines your character.

- Reputation is what you are supposed to be; character is what you are.
- Reputation is the photography; character is the face.
- Reputation comes over one from without; character grows from within.
- Reputation is what you have when you come to a new community; character is what you have when you go away.
- Your reputation is learned within an hour; your character does not come to light for a year.
- Reputation is grown like a mushroom; character grows like an oak.
- A single newspaper report gives you your reputation; a life of toil gives you your character.

- Reputation makes you rich or makes you poor; character makes you happy or makes you miserable.

- Reputation is what people say about you on your tombstone; character is what angels say about you before the throne of God.

- William Hersey Davis

What do you say to others by your words and/or actions?

Get Rid Of Your Junk

I once read in USA Today that American Airlines doesn't paint its jets because each pound adds $30 per year to fuel cost. Wouldn't that be cool if we would apply that principle to our very own lives? Things like holding grudges or having resentments would cost us extra each year. Someone once said, "Having a resentment is like taking poison and waiting for the other person to die."

It's crazy to think we can be the happy humans we all long to be and still hold on to the junk. We all know it is harder to travel with extra baggage. Why not follow the lead of American Airlines in the sense of getting rid of the extra weight. We would feel emotionally lighter and be less stressed. We would be a carefree group of individuals.

I know its tough, but it's us that complicate life. It's us that take on undue stress. It's that decision to hold on to resentment, gripes, grudges, and even guilt. This baggage only pulls us down, let it go. Ladies and gentlemen, let it go!! And soar higher than you have ever flown.

Magical Gem #50

Don't hold on to junk, gripes, grudges, and resentments. You only hurt yourself. And again, why would you want to do that? Be thankful that you do receive good things in your life.

> W.C. Fields once said, "Everyone believes in something. What do you believe in?"

The Power In Focusing Now!

The people that sell the beverage, Gatorade, wanted me to do a talk on How to Focus Better. What was I talking about? Oh yeah, focus. I talked with the big boss before the presentation and he said he wanted to bring me on in a very serious manner. I told him that I usually came on to the stage with some kind of joke accompanied by laughter. He insisted that he really wanted to fool the staff and let them think at first that I was a big boss or consultant or something serious. I agreed that we could do it his way, because that is what you do to thrive in business. You make the customer's wishes come true, not yours.

The presentation was the following day. I called my wife, Dede, and told her I was nervous because I was starting my talk in the morning on a serious note. She said, "What are you going to do?" I said, "I really don't know." I focused and thought to myself that there had to be a solution to this situation, a way to make us both happy. After a couple of hours, I came up with a fantastic solution. I could give the customer what they wanted and at the same time I could get what I wanted. I just hoped that the boss would go for the idea.

I called his hotel room and asked him if he could meet me in the lobby for ten minutes. Thankfully, he agreed. I informed him of my idea; he loved it, and said that he would play along with my scam.

This is what happened the following day. The boss introduced me and started with, "Notice the gentleman at the back of the room," and everybody turned around and looked at me. He continued, "You guys just happen to be looking at a gentleman that is going to help us immensely with our success. He's the youngest guy ever to graduate from Harvard University." A few of the guys mouthed the word "wow" as their heads began bobbing up and down. "He is a consultant to the Exxon Company as well as the Chief Financial Officer for the IBM Corporation. Here he is, Scott Francis."

The audience started clapping. Most of them still had their mouths open in awe of my credentials. They were impressed that I had accomplished all this at a young age. At this point, they were all thinking I was a pretty serious guy.

Without saying a word, I walked to the front of the room, put my briefcase on the table then opened it up. I looked up at them and said, "For the next three hours I will be talking about fungus." With that the big boss stood up at the back of the room and shouted, "I wanted you to talk about focus, not fungus!" All the heads in the audience popped up and looked at him. I said, "I thought you said 'fungus' a few weeks ago." He said, "No,

I said 'focus.'" After his comment, I said, "I don't have any thing prepared on focus." I closed my briefcase and said, "I am out of here."

The audience roared with laughter! They thought they had just witnessed one of the biggest screw-ups in history. Of course, it was all a big joke. It was a win-win situation. The boss got what he wanted, the serious introduction. I got what I wanted, the laugh. Everybody was happy. The talk went great and away I went.

You know, I was nervous starting my presentation like that. I was definitely outside my comfort zone. Fortunately, it worked out. With just a little creativity, a little thinking, and a little focus we can achieve anything we set our minds to.

I read one time that Michael Jordan made a comment about making a free throw. He said that if he focused on the ten million people watching him, he would miss his shot most of the time. If he focused in on just the basket and the task at hand, his shooting would improve and he would get the free throw most of the time.

In our lives it is so easy to get distracted by so many different things. We need to focus on what's important and achieve our goals. You see, I think fear sometimes sets in when we don't focus or concentrate and take our eyes off of the goal. If we would just focus more, we would double our personal effectiveness. We just need to train ourselves to learn to focus better. If you are like me, and I know I am, I do better when I'm not distracted. If you think about it, I mean really think about it, you can eliminate a lot of your distractions.

It's been said that one of the rarest things man does is try his hardest. What would you do if I told you there was one million dollars in cash waiting for you in New York in a briefcase that was in a locker and it was all legitimate with only one catch? The catch is that you would have to retrieve it within twenty-four hours. How many people would you allow to distract you with a conversation or trivial chit-chat? Would you take a two-hour lunch in the midst of your twenty-four hours? How about stopping to tell people about other things that are going on in your life? I think you would be booking a flight A.S.A.P. If you could not get a flight, you would be gassing up the car. Why? Because it would become a priority, and when we make things a priority we kick into a different gear, focus, and get the task done.

Magical Gem #51

If we make a task important enough, we will learn to focus and get much more done. Decide what's really important to you.

Respect, How to Get It

It was the biggest trade show in the world for the furniture industry. It was the High Point Furniture Market. Companies from all over the world gather for ten days to promote and sell their products. Clients attending to purchase inventory would be schmoozed with big name entertainment like Bill Cosby and Vanna White. I, myself, got to open up for the world famous Rich Little. That was pretty cool. It was an exciting ten days for High Point, which for the rest of the year is a slow-paced, out of the way, and quiet southern town.

I was hired in several venues to entertain various furniture groups. One time, I was working during a social hour. My job was to walk around doing close-up magic for a particular manufacturer. For another company, I might do a sales talk before the buyers arrived. Sometimes, I would work in the showroom. I would read in the corner waiting for a customer to show up. When a company arrived that was going to order from tens of thousands to millions of dollars worth of inventory, my job would be to break the ice with them. I was hired to make them laugh and to put them in a good mood. Lots of times the order would be double from last year partly due to their relaxed frame of mind from the laughter. I thought that company used my talents well. Oh, I almost forgot; I got paid well also.

One night I was invited to entertain a small group of guys at a really nice restaurant. I was to do close up magic for them. There were only fourteen of us at dinner. The attendees were the owner of a seventy million dollar a year company (this was eighteen years ago), me, and twelve of his top sales staff. It was an all male, very macho group. We needed some female influence for sure.

We ate dinner and were just about to finish our desserts when the owner looked at me and said loudly enough for all to hear, "I want my favorite magician in the whole world to have the last bite of my dessert." I think he was on some sort of power trip. I politely declined, "No thank you." He paused and looked at me as if I had disrespected him or something. He said, "You don't understand. I want you to take the last bite of my dessert, now." I said, "I'm full and I'd rather pass, but thank you anyway." It was turning out to be some sort of showdown. It had become a very awkward situation. Nobody at the table said a word. They were all his "yes" men and were scared to say anything, I think. The boss attempted a third time, "Are you refusing to take the last bite of my dessert?" I said, "I really am full and would get sick if I did." If eyes could kill, I think I would have died a horrible death. Again, nobody said anything. It was as if we were frozen in time. It was weird. So then he motions me over with his curled index finger and says, "Come closer." I leaned in to hear him. We were face to face and only a foot away from each other. He states, "You know, there are other magicians out there and you can be replaced like that" as he snapped his fingers. I instantly lost respect for him, and wasn't going to let him walk all over me. I motioned to him with my index finger and as he came close and we were once again face-to-face I said, "There are a lot more companies than there are magicians. So, in actuality you could also be replaced like that" as I snapped my fingers. With that I got up and headed for the men's room.

One of the guys followed me into the bathroom and said, "Don't worry about it, he's just had too much to drink." I said, "That might be true, but nobody walks all over me like he just tried to do." He said, "I understand." I went back to the table and the issue was dropped. Everyone was talking again at the table.

As we left the restaurant, the big boss said, "Can I talk with you a minute?" I said, "Sure." We stepped behind a van in the parking lot. Once he got me alone out of earshot of everyone else he said, "Don't you ever make me look bad in front of my men again." I said, "I'm going to say the same to you. Don't ever make me feel bad in front of your men. You are a seventy million dollar guy and can buy and sell me ten times over, but you will have respect for me or we will not ever work together again, period." He smiled and said, "I like you. You stood up for yourself and I admire that. By the way, some of my men won't even do that. I think they are afraid of me."

I had worked for that company for about ten years in a

row. After that night, I never worked for them again. The good feeling we had shared was gone, it just wasn't the same. I would rather work less and be respected then to have more money, but no respect. I have always thought if you want respect, then give respect. It's almost like a boomerang. Most of the time it just comes back to you.

Magical Gem #52

Respect is a funny thing. It can take years to earn; and only seconds to lose. Respect everybody. If you want respect, then give it freely. It's like a smile. If you smile, it tells the person that you are smiling at, that they are okay and that you respect them as a human being. Most of the time this attitude will come back to you in a positive way.

It's nice to be important, but it's more important to be nice.

The Blame Game

My wife, Dede, must have banged her diamond engagement ring against a table or something because one day she discovered that the diamond was loose. She took it off and put it in the jewelry box to be fixed one day. Months went by and I asked her, "Don't you miss wearing your ring?" She said a resounding, "Yes!" I said, "Why don't you send it to the jewelers?" She happened to be extremely busy at the time. I said, "Well, I don't like your putting it in your jewelry box, because if someone breaks in, it will be one of the first places they will look (I hate that we have to think like this, but it is a reality). She said, "What do you think I should do with it until I have it fixed?" I said, "I think you should hide it somewhere thieves wouldn't think to look. I mean we don't want to make it easier for them do we?" She said, "Okay, I'll hide it where they won't find it so easily."

We got busy with traveling and jobs and I forgot about the ring conversation. One night I was cleaning the kitchen, a very rare occurrence similar to a whale sighting – even more rare than that, an Elvis sighting.

No wait, that would be common. Okay, so I finished cleaning the kitchen.

A few days later Dede said to me, "Where is my ring?" I said, "I don't know. Where is it? Where did you hide it?" She said, "I wrapped it in a tissue, then put it in a plastic zip-lock baggie, then put it in the brand new snoopy dog bowl on top of the microwave." I said, "Was it a snack size baggie?" She said, "Yes." I said, "Ohmigosh, I think I threw that away about a week ago." She said, "Please tell me you're kidding." I said, "No I'm not. In all probability, it's at the city dump." She put a newspaper down on the floor and started to go through the trash in the kitchen. I said to her, "Honey, I think you are wasting your time. I think it's long gone." I said, "Why did you hide it like that?" She said, "You told me to hide it good and to not put it somewhere obvious." I replied, "I know, but you made it look like trash." She said, "I know, it's a really great hiding place, don't you think?" I said, "A little too good if you ask me." She said, "Did you throw it away?" I said, "It looked like garbage." She asked, "Why on Earth didn't you take the tissue out of the bag and feel to see if something was wrapped up inside?" I said, "I was afraid to touch it." She said, "You were afraid to touch it?" I said, "Yeah, I thought it was a booger rag." Dede just kept digging for the ring in the trash. I kept reiterating, "It's no use, I threw it away a week ago." She kept saying, "A little voice is telling me it's in here." Sure enough she found the ring at the very bottom of the trash. It turned out that it was only four days and not a week since the trash had been taken out. We got really lucky that it all worked out.

As far as the blaming is concerned, I was blaming her for making it look like trash. In reality, it was a great hiding place. It's just that if you have a hiding place like that, then we need to inform each other of the James Bond technique being used. She was blaming me for not checking inside the tissue (again, I thought it was a snot rag and I wasn't going to touch it, I knew that much). In reality, nobody was wrong, really. I thought it was trash and she was thinking what a great hiding spot. There really was no one to blame in this situation. As humans we tend to blame first when we should wait a minute and find out the deal. The deal really was nobody was wrong; we just needed to communicate a little better, that is all.

Magical Gem #53

Be slow to blame. If you blame and find out something different you feel like a fool. Find out the facts first. Look at the problem, but really concentrate on the solution. Little people blame, big people take the blame and offer solutions. I was impressed once when I witnessed a football player say, "My bad" during a superbowl game. He was a big man to take responsibility during one of the most important games of the season. Wow, what character.

Oh Woe Is Thee

Several years ago I had a lot going wrong in my life all at the same time. I had car trouble, my refrigerator went on the blink, the hot water heater needed to be replaced as did the Air Conditioner Unit, and to top it all off the mailbox fell over. It was a disasterous week. I couldn't believe it. Approximately fifteen things went wrong in a ten day period. It must have been some kind of record or something.

I was scheduled to speak in Tampa, Florida. The event was held at the Ritz Carlton Hotel. At the time that all the things were going wrong, I found myself staying at one of the best hotels in the world.

I only had $75 on me. I usually traveled with at least $250, but all the things that went wrong the previous week tapped me out. So, I only had $75 to eat on until I got home. I was eating a $28 cheeseburger from room service because a cab to the nearest restaurant cost $50. I could not believe I was sitting on the balcony looking at the water and the beach, eating the most expensive cheeseburger I have ever eaten in my life, and staying at one of the swankiest hotels in the world and yet that night I was feeling sorry for myself.

I was thinking about all the bad things that had happened to me in the past ten days and it was getting me blue. I had gone down in the elevator to get a newspaper for a trick I was going to perform the next day. Just when I was thinking how sorry I was feeling that all these things were going wrong in my life, I saw a man in a wheel chair with one arm and no legs.

My feeling sorry for myself flew out the window. I changed my tune, quick! One person in the hall said that the man in the wheelchair was a US Senator. I thought to myself, that man could have felt sorry for himself, but he didn't let that stop him. He became a United States of America senator. I noticed that he had a great sense of humor and looked pretty happy. Wow. I quickly stopped feeling sorry for myself.

You know, no matter how bad things seem to get, you can always find someone who has more challenges, more struggles, or is in a worse situation than you. The thing is we all have struggles and challenges to overcome. We should really concentrate on what we have and not what we don't have, on what we can do and not what we can't. We have way more than we think. The way I look at it today is if I can walk I'm having a good day. If I get to eat, that's a good day. In life things are going to happen. You just have to take it in stride. Be happy for what you have today. Tomorrow you might not have it.

Magical Gem #54

Just be thankful for what you have, period.

♦ This Isn't The Life I Ordered ♦

Getting One Over On You

It was a slow Monday at the Credit Union. I walked in and there were two tellers at the windows to my left and four customers in line. There was a total of five customers in line including me. About forty feet away and to my right, a woman was talking with the president of the bank. The line I was in was getting even shorter with only one customer in each teller's line. The woman was talking with the president for a total of about six to seven minutes. Finally, there was just one customer left in one of the teller lines. One of the tellers got freed up, looked at me the only one left in line, and said, "May I help you?" At this point the woman who was forty feet away yells out, "I was next!" and then runs up and jumps in front of me. Please understand; there were no other customers in line behind me. The woman I am speaking of was at least forty feet out of the line. She could have talked with the president probably less than thirty more seconds, and walked up to the teller station without waiting. It didn't make sense for her to jump in front of me.

It's just like when you are driving down the road going

fifty-five miles an hour with no one behind you, someone will pull out in front of you at twenty miles per hour forcing you to hit your brakes. Then one-hundred yards later they will pull into another driveway or street. They could have just waited the ten extra seconds, let you pass, then take their sweet time pulling out and getting where they had to go. It just doesn't make any sense.

Some people can't stand for other people to be ahead of them. They are small-minded. You just let it go and do not allow things like that to steal your serenity. People will steal it if you let them. Don't let it faze you. Just let it be like water that rolls off of a ducks back. You see, real success allows you to be positive even though you are surrounded by negative people. Success means you can love even when you are surrounded by hatred. You can do it. It just takes a little practice. Okay, okay, a lot of practice. I heard one person put it this way: you have to keep the trolls away from your goals.

Magical Gem #55

There are a lot of dream stealers out there. People that will try to get one over on you. Be like the palm tree in the storm, flex and "Let it go." It's not worth getting upset over. Now go be a happy human.

The Scorpion

This is a little story someone once told me out in a parking lot one night. It has helped me to pay more attention to who I hang out with and also who I avoid, thank you Sammy.

One day a turtle was getting ready to swim across the river. A scorpion stopped him and asked if he could catch a ride with the turtle to the other side. The turtle told the scorpion there was no way he would do it as the scorpion would sting him and he would die from the poison. The scorpion promised the turtle that he wouldn't sting him, for if he did then he would drowned. The turtle thought that made sense, and he finally agreed to take the scorpion on his back to the other side. The scorpion hopped onto the turtles back and away they went. Halfway across the river, the scorpion stung the turtle. The turtle asked, "Why did you do that? Now we are both going to die." The scorpion answered, "I had to, I am a scorpion. It's my nature."

The heaviest thing you can carry through this life is a grudge.
Anonymous

♦ This Isn't The Life I Ordered ♦

When I was 16 years old I saw this sign. I have kept it for 28 years. I love it because it works.

Life's Golden Rules

If you open it, close it.
If you turn it on, turn it off.
If you unlock it, lock it up.
If you break it, admit it.
If you can't fix it, call in someone who can.
If you borrow it, return it.
If you value it, take care of it.
If you make a mess, clean it up.
If you move it, put it back.
If it belongs to someone else and you want to use it, get permission.
If you don't know how to operate it, leave it alone.
If it's none of your business, don't ask questions.
If it ain't broke, don't fix it.
If it will brighten someone's day, say it.

Author -Unknown

We All Have The Same Wind

I love to play Disc Golf; it is one of the ways I like to get exercise as well as to have fun. For those who do not know what Disc Golf is, it's very much like golf in the sense of keeping score. The low score wins. It also has the same lingo like "driver and putting," but instead of a golf ball and clubs you use a disc, sort of like a Frisbee. The only thing with a disc is that you would not want to play catch with it. If one of these were to hit you in the head you would have to be rushed to the hospital. That is why you throw toward a disc catcher, not toward each other. I love playing the game with friends and family. It happens to be one of my favorite pastimes. However, I have a pet peeve; I do not like to play while it is windy. Some people don't mind. I did. I want the conditions to be almost perfect. I mean, who doesn't? Well, a lot like life, it is not always perfect.

One day I was playing with three of my brothers and complaining that the wind was a little rough. I said it was affecting <u>my game</u> and <u>my score</u>, and I didn't like it. After all, I would like to have a low score. I mentioned the wind a second and third time. Finally my brother,

Kirk (one of the more outspoken brothers), said, "Scott, you keep complaining about the wind, and how it affects your score. You say it as if the wind only affected your performance. Well, I have news for you, we all have the same wind." Then like a bolt of lightning the obvious struck me. We do all have the same wind. For some odd reason I was looking at it like it I was affected more than the others. I was taken back by the obvious. I don't know why I viewed it like that, but the fact is I did. My brother Kirk opened my eyes. I was complaining about something that affects every person on a windy day. Every human being that plays disc golf in the wind is affected. So I started to view it differently. I got less upset at my worst scores because everybody had bad scores in the wind…duh!

It started me thinking on other things like: as humans we all have twenty-four hours a day, seven days a week. Why are some people rushed, while some seem like they have all the time in the world. I guess it's how we view things. It's how we prioritize. It's like putting only ten pounds of things to do in a ten-pound bag instead of trying to put twenty-five pounds of things to do in a ten-pound bag (which I often do). If you make everything important, then nothing is important. It's how you look at situations. It's finding your balance and not complaining about how bad the wind is, so to speak. It's making the necessary changes, viewing things in a different light. A light that if found will make you grow wiser, happier, and healthier.

We all have the same wind. It's what you do with that

wind that matters. When you are sailing out in the ocean there is no way you are going to change the wind, right? So change your sail and use the wind to your advantage. It's not the wind; it's what you do with that wind that really matters.

Since that time, I have literally played in all types of not so perfect conditions including rain, wind, and even snow. I'm not joking. I don't care what the conditions are. We are going to have fun…even if our scores are less than perfect.

Magical Gem #56

We all have the same conditions we are given 24 hours a day, 7 days a week, and 365 days a year. The same conditions apply to us all, yet some accomplish more. Stop complaining of your conditions and make good things happen.

Pre-Judging People

The year was 1977. I was seventeen years old and had entered a talent show in Winston Salem, NC. It was a pretty big show with six hundred people in attendance. Entered in the show were lots of singers and musicians. I was the only comic-magician. I thought that was a good position to be in, because I was different than the other talent. Maybe I would stand out from the crowd and this would give me an edge. The show went on for two hours, and then it was finally my turn. I got on stage, made the audience laugh big time, and then sat down. I figured that I had first place in the bag. As a teenager, being young and cocky was my job. I asked the coordinator who else had to perform. He informed me there was only one singer left. I smiled to myself, because I just knew I was going to win the contest for sure. As I looked over at the last performer, an older heavy set lady, I was thinking to myself, "What could she possibly do to win the contest?" Please keep in mind that I was only seventeen and was young and dumb, not to mention cocky.

The lady got up on stage and sang the Barbara Streisand song, "People". As the lady sang the most beautiful version I had ever heard sung, "People…people who need people are the luckiest people in the world…," tears were running down my face. I realized I was a big jerk. I had prejudged her talent based on her appearance, long before I knew anything about her.

I know I learned a big lesson that night. The lesson I learned was NEVER to prejudge anyone. There is no way of knowing what people are capable of doing, just by looking at them. I am so glad I learned that at seventeen I really don't remember who won the contest, but I have never forgotten her rendition of that song. The contest was insignificant next to the sound of that lady's voice in the lesson that was learned.

Magical Gem#57

Prejudging others based on appearances is shallow and lacks character. Not only could we miss out on the experience of a life time, but we could cheat ourselves out of deep and meaningful relationships with others whose appearance is less than perfect. Look beyond what is seen. Look with your heart to the true spirit of the individual.

Turn Dreams Into Reality

Wouldn't that be the bomb if you were more successful than you ever dreamed possible? It can and will be if you allow it to be. Say for instance you spent less time wondering whether certain people liked you or not, and more time enjoying the simple fact that it doesn't really matter. Wouldn't that be better? If you put lots of little ideas like this together, your life would be a lot better, right? The bottom line is that you reach your full potential. Wouldn't that just be awesome? When we change to a positive attitude, we achieve daily victories that add up to an all around better life. Ann Landers put it this way, "Look at the problem, now substitute the word opportunity." This idea alone would catapult your life exponentially to the good. You know dreams do come true if you work diligently toward them. So prepare for greatness. You might just get that fairy tale ending. I know one thing, if the principles in this book are applied on a daily basis, you will absolutely, no question about it, change your life. Do you hope for success or are you committed to success? Follow through; discover the wonder of you and make great things happen. Give life your all. You will grow and prosper and become the person you were meant to be.

Magical Gem #58

My goal of writing a book only took twenty years. No, I am not kidding. I really want to get this across; if this 'C' and 'D' dyslexic student can make an impossible dream possible, I promise with all of my being, you can too. This could be your finest hour. The time is now!!

Well done is better than well said
-Benjamin Franklin

True Friends

I feel that I am a millionaire when it comes to friends. I have some great friends all over the country and they are all so different from one another. That is what makes life fun and interesting.

I asked one friend, "would you take a bullet for me if you had to?" He said, "Yes, I would, but not in the chest." We both laughed out loud. I have some friends that I call every day. Then there are others that I only get to talk to once every few months or so. We pick up right where we left off. Friends encourage you to do and be your very best. A friend is someone who really cares. A true friend listens and knows when you are down. Nothing can take the place of a good friend. They seem to know when to cheer you up. They know when you are blue and need a joke or two. It's invaluable to have good relationships with friends, because with true friends you can be yourself and not have to put on a front. My wife is my best friend. I feel better even if she's in the house. Just knowing she's close by makes me feel good, even if we don't talk. She said one time to her friend on the phone, "Scott and I love to talk. We love sometimes not talking.

Sometimes I think we could not talk forever." That was funny. I love laughing with my friends. It is good to have friends you can count on, especially if you are moving. Just kidding!!

Magical Gem #59

Friends can enhance your life. Just make sure they are the right friends. If they drag you down, they are not true friends.

There's very little difference between people, but that little difference makes a big difference.
-W. Clement Stone

Misunderstandings

#1 One Sunday afternoon, I was reading the newspaper when my five year old niece asked me if I would read the cartoons to her. The cartoon was of Ziggy, standing on the front stoop of his house with a big black rain cloud over his head. The caption read, "Do you believe in omens?" My niece responded, "Yes, I do." I was shocked that a five year old could grasp the concept of an omen. I said, "Nicole, you believe in omens?" She said, "Yes!" I said, "Okay, tell me what an omen is." She said, "Well, there are peanuts, cashews, and omens (almonds)."

#2 Another time my wife and I decided to purchase a couch. The company called and left a message on our answering machine. The message said, "Your Rowe's couch (the name of the brand) is in." My wife said to me, "We are NOT taking a "rose" couch. We ordered a white couch and we are not accepting a rose one." I said, "Honey, 'Rowe's' is the name of the brand." She said, "Oh."

#3 One night my mom was watching a hockey game on TV. The next day the neighbor asked, "Are you okay?" My mom replied, "Yes, why?" The neighbor said, "It sounded like maybe your husband was hitting you, I heard you yelling 'No, no, no!' last night." My mom laughed and said, "I was watching my favorite hockey team and cheering them on with 'Go, go, go!'"

#4 One time I was entertaining a Japanese crowd. The gentleman on stage said something and everyone in the audience clapped including me. I not only clapped, I clapped and whistled. One of the Japanese gentlemen leaned over and said, "He was introducing you." Yes, I was embarrassed.

#5 I called a company one day and asked the young receptionist, "Would you get that message to the boss?" She said, "I will be happy to delay the message." I said, "You mean relay the message, right?" She said, "Relay, delay, whatever."

#6 I was a young guy and had just attended a presentation by a wonderful professional speaker. I was in awe of his professionalism. After the program, I went up and shook his hand and said, "You…you…you…" I could not think of an appropriate word. "You …reek with professionalism." He smiled real big and said, "I wouldn't necessarily use the word reek." Of course, I knew I said something stupid. I was the comedian and had to fix the situation quickly. I said, "No, your really do have a professional stench about you." Then we both laughed.

#7 My father-in-law, Jack snores loudly when he sleeps on his back. One night his wife, Jean said, "Jack, get on your side." So, he scooted over to his side of the bed. Again, Jean said, "Jack, get on your side." He scooted a little closer to the edge of the bed. A third time Jean said, "Jack, get on your side." He sat up in bed and said, "Jean, if I move any farther onto my side, I am going to fall off the bed!" She replied, "No, turn on your side, you're snoring again."

I shared with you seven little scenarios that all had some kind of misunderstandings in them. Those types of misunderstandings can happen to any of us because words are sometimes misinterpreted. I would like to propose that we give others the benefit of the doubt. Perhaps they just misunderstood your request or got confused. Make sure you are clear in communicating your request by keeping it simple.

Magical Gem #60

Be absolutely clear in your ideas and requests. Have the other person repeat back what you've said to make sure they got the message clearly. Good communication can benifit you greatly.

***Katherine Graham once said...
To love what you do and feel
that it matters how could
anything be more fun?***

Why Me?

During this particular time in my life I was not being dealt a good hand. Lots of personal crises were happening. The most impactful to me was the death of my father. In addition to that one of my friends left his wife of many years. I was really getting angry. I would constantly ask, "Why me?" Why is this happening me or my dad or my friends.

Have you ever asked yourself, "Why me?" Liar!! Or, did you answer yes? Okay then. Seriously, did you ever break down in a car or hurt yourself accidently and say, "Why me? Why is all this happening to me?" Even smaller, yet still bothersome things were happening. For example, they stopped making my favorite candy bar. Out of all the candy bars on the shelf, they had to stop making my favorite one. Good grief! I like a certain toothpaste. One night I went to the grocery store looking for my favorite toothpaste in a small tube because I travel a lot and don't feel like lugging around extra toothpaste. The smaller tube fits in my toiletry bag better. I'm not kidding when I say, out of twenty-four choices of toothpaste within the same brand, (the SAME EXACT brand) they chose the size I like and stopped making it!! The one that works out perfectly for my bag!! I think I made my point.

We all have frustrations and disappointments big or small at times in our lives. Sometimes a friend treats us poorly. These things can't be figured out. So, when I am perplexed at something that has gone wrong, or feel that a person has wronged me, or whatever it is, I just say, "It is what it is!" and just leave it at that. If you don't, you will drive yourself crazy. Don't try to solve all the puzzles.

Magical Gem #61

Truly, "It is what it is." Accept life, embrace it, and you won't get frustrated with it.

You manage things. You lead people.

"Love It" Technique

Did you ever in your life have something go wrong? Like you bend over and your sunglasses drop on the ground. As you bend over to pick them up, the pen or something else drops, or spills, or falls. Or the computer crashes or, or, or. Well most people curse in those circumstances. I have discovered, I think, a better way to have fun and be a little crazy and unique as a healthy alternative to cursing. I say out loud, (like you really do) "I LOVE IT!!" Then I will look around and ask people, "Did you just see that? That landed perfectly. If it wasn't for the ground, that would have kept going, I love it!! Look how perfectly that drink spilled, I absolutely LOVE it." People always laugh at this and ask, "Do you really love that?" I always say, "No, but it's better than the alternative."

Magical Gem #62

I'm telling you, this sounds crazy, but I am happier when I use this technique. Try it, you will love it!

What's Important to You?

Sometimes learning lessons can be fun. I promised my seven year old niece, Keegan, I would take her to play Frisbee/Disc golf with me. We drove to the park and pulled into a spot right in front of the swings, monkey bars, and slides. I said, "I am really excited to bring you to play Frisbee golf with me." She pointed at the playground and said, "But they have swings and stuff." I said, "I know, but we're headed to play Frisbee golf." Again she pointed and said, "But they have swings and slides." After hearing it a second time, I finally said, "Well, okay, do you want to go on the playground instead?" She squealed, "Yeah!" I almost missed the clues. People are interested in what they are interested in, and that's okay. Am I glad I heard her loud and clear. That was a day filled with great big smiles and wonderful memories.

Magical Gem #63

When we listen to what others want, we make people happy. When we make people happy, we ourselves are happier

The great thing in this world is not so much where we are, but in what direction we are moving.
-Oliver Wendell Holmes

Be Careful Where You Get Your Information

One day in an Indian village, the elders in the group approached a warrior and said, "We have decided that you will be our next chief." He was all excited and honored at being chosen. They said, "The chief will train you for the next year." The next day the old chief dropped dead. The tribe approached the warrior and said, "Okay, you are the chief, what do we do now?" He said, "I don't know what to do." They asked, "Should we gather wood for the winter?" Thinking this was a good idea, he said, "Okay, yeah, gather wood for the winter." The next day he just wanted to make sure he was giving the right info, so he called the weather station and asked them, "Are we going to have a bad winter?" They said, "Yes." He returned to the tribe and said, "We need to gather more wood, we are going to have a bad winter." So the tribe gathered more wood. The new chief wanted to make absolutely certain that this was right, so he called the weather station again. He asked them, "Is it going to be a really severe winter?" They said, "Yes." Again, he went back to the tribe and told them to gather even more wood. So finally the new chief called the weather station and asked them, "How do you guys know if the winter is going to be bad?" The guy at the weather station said, "We just watch to see how much wood the Indians gather."

***People are sometimes
unaware of the path
they are on...
the path of truth is
the most narrow.***

Clean Jokes You Can Tell

A Gentleman Name Trevor From Whales Told Me This One...

An executioner was going to execute three prisoners. He was in a good mood and told them that if they could sing a song about a dog, he would let them go. He approached the first prisoner and said, "Do you have a song?" The prisoner started singing, "How much is that doggie in the window?" The executioner said, "You can go." He asked the second prisoner about his song. He sang, "You ain't nothin' but a hound dog." He said, "You can go." He approached the third prisoner and said, "What's your song about a dog?" The prisoner thought for a minute and then sang, "Strangers in the night...Exchanging glances...Strangers in the night..." The executioner said, "What the heck does that have to do with a dog?" The prisoner said, "Listen to the rest of the song...Scooby dooby doo..."

There was a NY City hot dog vendor selling hot dogs. A man came up and asked for one. The vendor gave the man a hot dog and recieved a $20 bill. The vendor opened up his money box, threw in the $20, and went back to work. The man said, "Where is my change?" The hot dog vendor said, "Your change must come from within."

Put everything you've got into everything you do.

First Impressions

Whether you are in sales, customer service, or just plain want to make a great first impression, this story is for you. Some people do not realize the importance of this next subject. I can't tell you how many times I have gone to shake someone's hand only to discover they are hiding a limp noodle under their sleeve. A hand shake is supposed to be moderately firm, but not forceful. A handshake should not be so firm as to dominate. One little guy tried to twist my wrist off! I think there were different issues there. Be firm with women, as well, unless they are wearing lots of rings. Then be a little less firm, so you don't hurt them. Don't give a finger shake, either. The skin that stretches between your thumb and index finger should meet. At the same time look the person right in the eye, smile, and shake.

Magical Gem #64

A firm handshake, good eye contact, and a smile are all important elements of a great first impression. It surprizes me me how many people, even sales people, that still don't know how to shake hands well.

Unstoppable

Can't is such an ugly word, isn't it? don't you hate when one person discourages another by a stupid little phrase like, "You can't do it. It will never work," or even, "It can't be done!" I think it is an old Chinese Proverb that states: a man trying to tell another man it can't be done should never get in the way of another man that's doing it.

Here are two short stories about people I personally know that in my opinion didn't have a chance of succeeding under their conditions, but succeeded anyway. Boy I am glad I kept my mouth shut. Now, here's what belief and a little passion mixed, with get up and go, can do for you.

In the first story we'll call this guy Wayne, because that's his name. Wayne said to me, "You know, I am going to start a photography business." I said, "That's great. What type of camera do you have?" He said, "I don't have a camera. I can borrow one from my neighbor." I thought, my friend has no camera, no money; he has just adopted three kids, and is a stay at home Dad. Was I crazy to think the odds were against this guy? But

I wasn't going to step on anybody's dream, that's for sure! If he thought he could do it, wow, more power to him. So my friend, Wayne, borrowed his neighbors camera, went to the park, and started taking pictures of trees, flowers, his kids, etc, etc. People with other kids asked him if he was a professional photographer. He would just say he was starting a business and didn't have any business cards on him. However, he would write down their number and set up a photo session. Other times, as he was taking pictures in the park, he would tell moms and dads that they had beautiful children and comment that maybe sometime he could shoot their kids. Well, not "shoot" them, but actually take some shots of them.

You see, with the combination of his passion for taking pictures and his commitment to bring money into his household, he was unstoppable. He was on track to succeed and apparently was going to do just that. From time to time I would get updates. A few days or a week would go by, and each time I was amazed at this guy and what was happening. Within weeks of starting a photo business on a BORROWED camera, did I mention BORROWED camera, he was getting booked a bunch. At this time he wasn't even that good with the camera yet. It still didn't stop him or even slow him down. He was on a path, his path to success. I was in awe and was excited for him. I mean who wouldn't pull for this guy? He was an underdog.

Even though he was a highly intelligent man, the odds of him succeeding were stacked against him. Come on now, no camera, stay at home dad with three toddlers!

The kids alone are a full time job. Before you knew it, he was booked solid for the next two to three months! He accomplished this first phase in only eight to twelve weeks, folks! Believe it or not, Wayne was hungry for more. He enlarged his photos to eleven and a half by seventeen and a half for easy viewing and started calling on Public schools with his kids literally by his side. He would hold the three year olds hand, strap one twin on his back and carry the other twin, as well as cart his portfolio full of pictures in his other arm.

Now, if you told ninety-nine percent of people or even highly motivated salesmen that those were the conditions they would have to sell in, if they didn't faint first, they would at the very least look at you like you had two heads and probably say something like, "You are kidding me, right?" The fact of the matter is that Wayne is in that one percentile. His commitment, his passion, and his purpose made him unstoppable. Two years later Wayne has fifteen employees, has purchased a one-hundred-thousand dollar piece of equipment, and operates out of a twenty-three-hundred square foot office. He also does commercial work and has more business than he knows what to do with. And he does tens of thousands of dollars worth of business per month. I don't know how far Wayne will go with his photography business. Whatever he does, he will succeed, because when you are one-hundred-fifty percent committed to your cause, you are unstoppable. I wish my amazing friend Wayne all the best.

The difference between ordinary and extraordinary is that little extra.
          -Unknown

Unstoppable Story # 2: Dave From Savannah

(The Power of Passion)

One Friday night, I was headlining a comedy club in Savannah, GA. After the show a young guy, about seventeen years old, approached me, stuck out his hand and said, "Hey, I'm Dave from Savannah and I do magic too!" I said, "That's great Dave (smiled), if you will excuse me I have to repack my props for the show for tomorrow night." He said, "That's okay, can I just talk to you while you pack?" Now most people would have taken that as an indication that I was busy and had to pack and would prefer to do it alone. Not Dave. He was on a mission. He wanted, as he mentioned, to pick my brain (that's how we all learn magic tricks, from other magicians). I sensed he was on a life mission and wanted to learn the ropes. He continued to ask how it was to do show on the road, etc.

Dave and I became friends over time, and I told him to call me anytime. Anyone that has a passion or a dream and loves performing magic that much, I wanted to help. I love magic and performing and I knew Dave from Savannah did too. His passion drove him to call me every few months to give me an update. One night I got a call, "Scott, this is Dave from Savannah. I am saving my money to take a bus to Las Vegas to meet Lance Burton."

(If you aren't familiar with Lance Burton I will tell you about him. Lance is a mega success story. He went to Las Vegas with nothing and a few years later he signed a contract for one-hundred million dollars over thirteen years.)

So, Dave from Savannah thinks he is going to meet this famous magician. My first though was that he wouldn't even get close to this guy. But again, who am I to step on anyone's dream? I wished him luck and told him to be careful. A few months later I was teaching at a magic convention in Columbia, SC and Dave from Savannah showed up. He told me he went to Las Vegas to meet Lance Burton. I was expecting him to say he approached Lance and Lance blew him off, or security led him out of the building with his feet doing a levitation bit as he was being carried out. Instead, Dave's dream came true. He said, "I got to hang out with Lance." At this point I was leaning forward on my chair as I was so excited for Dave. He continued, "Okay, I went to Las Vegas and attended Lance's show. Afterwards, I was hanging out in the magic shop where they sell souvenirs. A clerk in the magic shop asked me if I enjoyed the show. I said yes, very much. He asked me what other shows I was going to see while I was in Vegas. I explained to the clerk my sole purpose for coming to Vegas was to meet

Lance Burton. I told him how I saved my money and took a bus there, hoping I would get to meet Lance. At this point the clerk smiled and said that Lance Burton was his dad. He told me there was a magic meeting the next night and that his dad, Lance Burton would pick me up in the parking lot. The next day as Lance Burton, the one-hundred million dollar magician pulled up in a white corvette to pick me up for the magic meeting!" At this I was in awe. Not at the fact that he got to meet Lance, but at the fact that he, Dave from Savannah, had a dream and pursued it and it came to pass. His dream was fulfilled. I admire Dave from Savannah. There are more talented, older, and smarter magicians than Dave, but they are guys that will never ever take a chance on their dreams. Why? Because they don't believe or don't have a passion or even any commitment toward their very own dreams. Thanks young, Dave, for inspiring me, and hopefully others.

Magical Gem #65

Believe in your dreams and your passions, but most of all believe in yourself!!

The Big Cover Up

My wife, Dede, and I were enjoying ourselves in our back yard, when every few minutes, we would get attacked by wasps swarming around our heads

We couldn't figure out where they were coming from. It was not a lot of fun ducking and dodging and trying not to get stung. Finally I decided to put on my Sherlock Holmes cap and investigate. I sat still on a chair and observed. They were coming from a scrap pile of wood leftover from an old deck. I uncovered the wood pile and there it was, a big nest right in the center! I sprayed the nest and broke it apart . The problem was solved.

It reminded me of problems that we deal with in our home and our work lives. If we ignore the problem, it seems to get worse. When we uncover and deal with our issues, it's usually not that bad. As for me, I'm going address the problems that I face head on. As Barney Fife used to say on the Andy Griffith Show, "<u>Andy, we need to nip it in the bud!</u>"

Magical Gem #67

Problems in life can be difficult. I really have found, at least in my life, that it's important to face issues head on. It's hard to do that sometimes, but better in the long run if you do.

We don't stop playing because we grow old, we grow old because we stop playing.

Anonymous

You don't drowned by falling in water. You drowned by staying in the water.

-Calvit Roberts

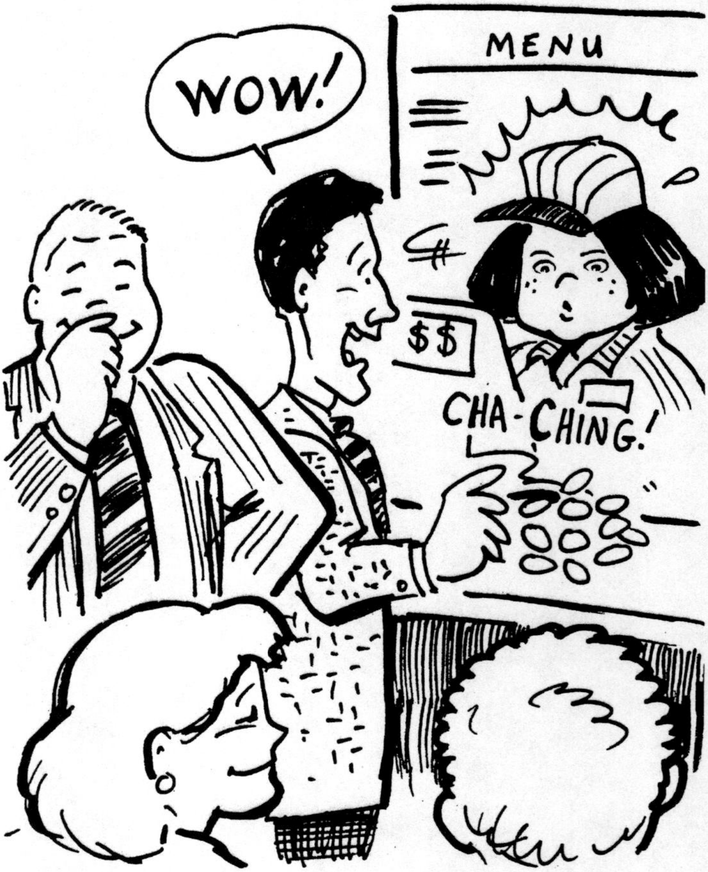
MENU
WOW!
$$
CHA-CHING!

Humor With A Purpose #3

I wanted to get rid of a lot of extra change that had accumulated in the ashtray in my van. I happened to be meeting a friend of mine for lunch. Standing in line at the fast food place I noticed that the cash register had one of those attachments that the change slides down and lands in a bowl. My friend ordered and paid for his lunch first. He was only supposed to get thirty-seven cents back in change. As the cashier was looking at the register keys, I threw about eight dollars worth of change into the bowl and acted as though I had hit the jackpot. I said, "Wow!" As I started to scoop the change out of the bowl, the girl panicked, grabbed my wrist, and said, "<u>I think I must have hit a wrong button.</u>" All the customers in the line behind us cracked up laughing. Including the girl at the register, once she got the scoop on the joke. The laughter got the attention of the manager. He walked over and asked what was going on. I explained that we were just having fun with life. He said, "We don't usually get that kind of attitude from the customers, did you pay for lunch yet?" I said, "No, I haven't." He said, "Well, lunch is on me!" I don't do these crazy antics for the free lunch. But, if they are going to insist, that's fine with me!

♦ This Isn't The Life I Ordered ♦

Humor With A Purpose #4

I like to joke around a lot. Am I able to get serious? Yes if I have to. I think that some people take themselves too seriously. I was flying out of town for one of my speaking presentations and decided to have some fun. I took a pair of toy glasses that had springs coming out of the lenses and bulging bloodshot discs at the end of the springs for eyes. I popped the discs off, placed them over my own eyes, and squinted my eyes to hold them in place. As I was saying some people are too serious, especially at the airport. With the bulging bloodshot discs covering my own eyes I stepped up to the counter at the departure gate, pointed to a plane taking off the runway, and said, "Is that my plane?" All the gate agents started laughing. I have been bumped from coach to first class dozens of times because of this little joke. I don't do it for a free upgrade, but if it happens...well, okay!

Magical Gem #68

Laugh a lot to invest in your health. If other people benefit as a byproduct, that's great. I plan to laugh as much as possible for the rest of my days.

♦ This Isn't The Life I Ordered ♦

"*They're yours free and clear!*"

Humor With A Purpose #5

I like creative salespeople. This story is about a guy that sells used cars for a living, expensive used cars. We all know that moment right before the customer signs the contract for the car is tense. This creative salesman, at the height of that moment, breaks the tension by throwing a set of fuzzy dice on the desk while saying, "If you sign right now, I'll throw in a set of these." This is a brilliant idea. Before you laugh too much at his silliness you should know, he is the number one salesman at his company!

Magical Gem #69

If you can use humor in an unusual way to break up a tense situation, by all means do! There is only one time I think humor isn't good or appropriate. If there is malice behind the joke, don't do it. Happy Jestering.

Attitude Is Everything

Sea World is a wonderful place. I was visiting a few years ago with my mom and my wife, Dede. We were all having a fantastic time, when suddenly the Budweiser horses and carriage came by with the Budweiser song playing in the background. There was a guy following the cart with a broom and dust pan. He was whistling and almost dancing, he was so happy.

Take a guess at what his job was. Yep!, You guessed it.! He cleaned up after the horses, a job most people would not enjoy much. I told my wife I just have to talk to this guy to find out what his secret is.

I asked the man if I could ask him a question. He said "OK."

I said, "I mean no disrespect whatsoever, but how is it that you are so happy with this kind of job? His response was, "Well, I get to work outside, in shorts, and, they pay me decent. But most of all, I feel I clean up after the finest horses on earth". "WOW", I said. That was his secret. His attitude was top notch toward what he did.

♦ Now What? ♦

Magical Gem #70

If a guy can have a job like that, and still feel that great, then the secret to your life and your job is your attitude towards it.

Give me one person 100% committed to their purpose rather than ninety-nine people who are halfway.

Give life your ALL and you <u>will</u> become the person you were meant to be.

Scott Francis